D1075435

THE THINKING
JEWISH TEENAGER'S
GUIDE TO
LIFE

THE THINKING JEWISH TEENAGER'S GUIDE TO LIFE

Akiva Tatz

TARGUM/FELDHEIM

First published 1999

Printing plates by Frank, Jerusalem

Published by:
Targum Press Inc.
22700 W. Eleven Mile Rd.
Southfield, Mich. 48034

in conjunction with
Mishnas Rishonim

Distributed by:
Feldheim Publishers
200 Airport Executive Park
Nanuet, N.Y. 10954

Distributed in Israel by:
Targum Press Ltd.
POB 43170
Jerusalem 91430

Printed in Israel

The publication of this book
has been made possible
by the generosity of

David and Judith Lobel

of New York

People of
Vision and Initiative
in Building a Jewish Future

From Rabbi Moshe Shapira's recommendation; (translated):

The Sages say that only one who grasps wisdom in its depth can transmit it suitably to the understanding of youth.
Rabbi Akiva Tatz has undertaken to present aspects of Torah wisdom and to convey something of its depth.
His words should be studied closely, for they emanate from the deep wellsprings of Torah.
It is to be hoped that they shall be so studied and that they bear fruit in the hearts of those who study them.

Rabbi Moshe Shapira.

This is a thought-provoking book which examines some of the most important elements of Jewish thought and practice.
Our generation is characterized by superficiality and lack of genuine Jewish knowledge; this book addresses both.
I would recommend that Jews of all ages study these pages; herein they will find keys to many of life's challenges and wonders.

Rabbi Mordechai Miller
Principal, Jewish Teachers' Training College

בס״ד

Acknowledgments

This book has been written to provide young Jewish adults with an approach to life's most important issues from an authentic Jewish perspective. Each subject discussed here is of immediate and real application to life and should be integral to any young person's evolving set of values and principles.

In each area, the Jewish attitude and understanding is discussed and contrasted with that of the culture which surrounds us.

The ideas dealt with here are presented in depth and require thought; the aim is to challenge the reader to think creatively, originally and to develop an intelligent approach to life informed by genuine Jewish values.

It is my hope that in addition to teenagers, those who have progressed beyond that age will explore the material presented here and find that they too have the suppleness of mind to re-examine their values and visions.

* * *

Sources are not attributed directly in the text. Most of the material herein is presented as I was privileged to learn it from Rabbi Moshe Shapira, and essentially all of my ability to understand it to any degree is due to him. He has opened a world to this generation; this book represents a small part of that wellspring.

Some material is Rabbi Dessler's; much of that is expressed through the medium of the teaching of Rabbi Mordechai Miller.

The following people provided essential assistance and I thank them:

* My mother, Mrs. Minde Tatz, for her usual meticulous work on the manuscript;
* David and Judith Lobel for their gracious support;
* Rabbi Professor David Gottlieb. His sharp eye and demanding standards for logic and clarity have been invaluable;
* Ruth and Tamar Tatz, Rachel Naomi and Rivka Leah Karnowsky, Jonathan and Anna Goldberg for their close reading of the manuscript. Their comments and suggestions added immeasurably;
* Gavriel Tatz for his creative and technical assistance;
* The staff of Targum Press for their exceptional efficiency and patience. Working with them continues to be a pleasure;
* My wife Suzanne, an incomparably greater guide to life than anything I could write.

A.T.
Sivan 5759
June 1999

Contents

Introduction

Who are you? What are your values? What are your ambitions? What makes you different? What is unique about you?

Defining your role in life requires some thinking about your personality and your values. What is important to you? What impresses you? Are you impressed by the same things that impress others? If your desires and ambitions are similar to those of most members of the society around you, have you thought about your values consciously and chosen them for yourself?

Most people accept the norms and values of the society in which they find themselves. Most people want the same things that others want. Most people are products of their society and their environment. Most people follow; they do not think things out for themselves.

But that is not the Jewish way. Judaism is a life path that requires thinking. Judaism requires the courage to think powerfully about values and it requires the courage to reject values despite their acceptance by society at large. We accept values because they are right, not because the world around us does. And we reject values when they are wrong, even if the whole world believes in them.

Abraham was ready to stand against an entire world. His values were thought out and consciously chosen, and they were not those of his society or his generation. Ever since then, that has been our way.

We live in a society that does not think Jewishly. In many ways the ideas and values of the society around us are completely opposed to those of Judaism. We live in society and we absorb its values, its norms and its thoughts. We see through the eyes of a culture, but that culture is not ours.

What does Judaism teach about life's issues and where does that teaching differ from the ideas and values of the culture around us? Do you have the tools to acquire that knowledge? What part of the pattern of your thinking is Jewish?

We need to see things as they are. We need to think clearly and objectively. We need to do the very hard work of clarifying how much of our mind is really ours and how much is the residue of a culture and an age, how much is our own original thought and how much is the passively absorbed material of a worldview that is not ours.

Do you have the courage to do that? Can you handle the challenge of looking at yourself honestly and fearlessly? Will you be able to give up those views and values that turn out to be false even if they have been dear to you until now? Can you look at Judaism's depth and see it through pure eyes, and then turn those eyes on a complex world and see through its illusions?

Can you look deeply into yourself and face what you find?

Chapter 1

Free Will - the Real You

The most important thing to grasp about being human is the fact that you have free choice. *You* make the decisions. *You* are responsible. We shall attempt to show that the secular world is not so sure about this, but as a Jew, you have to know that everything significant about life depends on this idea.

Let us explore the concept of free will and understand why it is essential in coming to grips with who you really are.

What are the components of human free will and what are its limits?

Free will applies only in the area of morality. That is, you are free only when it comes to decisions and actions which relate to your personal battle when you are tempted to do that which is immoral. Only in the arena of the battle between good and evil are you free to win or lose. Only when you are challenged with a situation in which you can act as you know you should, in line with your higher self, and at the same time you are tempted by the more physical, the more sensuous and animalistic, can you apply your free will and battle the ordeal.

You have very little free choice outside the area of morality. Your health, wealth and many other areas of life have large components which cannot be controlled no matter how you try. But in moral tests, you are entirely in control. That is where you are free.

Of course there are many things outside the realm of morality which you can choose, but those choices are purely technical: certainly you can choose a particular flavor of ice cream, for example, or which socks you will wear today; but those choices are not uniquely human. Animals also choose options like which food to eat and where to sleep; those areas have no inner meaning, they are mechanical issues. Here we are talking about the unique free will of human beings, that faculty which makes you unlike any animal. The area in which animals *cannot* make any choices is the area of morality. No animal chooses between right and wrong; no animal battles to overcome its lower self and achieve a more spiritual state by means of its moral ordeals. That is exactly the area we mean when we talk of human free will; the battleground of human free will is precisely the area of moral ordeals, the striving for higher values against the pull of our lower selves.

How free are you? What is the nature of this freedom? What about someone who has tremendous disadvantages outside of his or her own making – disadvantages of upbringing, emotional problems, lack of natural talents, financial limitations or anything else which seems to make personal progress difficult? Do we say that such a person has less free will? Do we say that such a person is less accountable for his or her moral failures? Perhaps such a person is not accountable at all?

This requires some thought. Let us study the interaction between free will and those things which affect it.

Many factors affect your area of free will; in fact, many factors outside of your free will determine what your ordeals will be, and how difficult those ordeals will be. But the critical issue to understand is that at the moment of ordeal, *at the point of choice itself,* you are entirely free. You may find yourself in a particular test through no fault of your own, through causes and events entirely outside your control. *But how you respond in that test is entirely up to you.*

Each person has a point of free will which is determined by many factors. In fact, in various areas of life you may have very different levels of free will; some types of ordeal may be much more difficult for you whereas for someone else other types of ordeal may provide greater challenges. You may not be tempted by things which someone else can hardly resist, and yet you may have a mighty struggle with things which would be a walkover for that person. In fact, some tests may be exceedingly difficult for one person and be *virtually out of the realm of free choice* for someone else.

And not only that: some things in your own life may be intensely difficult to overcome while others do not even present a challenge. And exactly which areas are difficult and which are not may be constantly changing. Let us analyze this.

Your battle of free choice takes place only at your point of free choice. In any area of your life which involves moral issues, you have a point at which you are being tested. Below that point, things are so easy that they are not really tests; you would not fail there because you are too powerful. You always succeed there because you handle those things correctly *out of habit* – in short, they are not tests at all.

Above that point, you are not being tested either: things above your point of free choice are too difficult for you; you do not handle those things correctly because you are too weak. You are not yet ready to grapple with things at those higher levels; you fail there without doing battle. The experiences of those levels are not your tests either.

An extreme example will illustrate this idea: imagine an individual who is morally undeveloped; someone whose life consists of gross violence and physicality. Say, an individual who mugs helpless victims daily and has been doing so ever since he was a youth brought up in desperate circumstances. This criminal has a very low point of free choice – his maximum moral choice may be whether to apply more or less violence the next time he mugs a frail old woman or not.

Now if this individual decides to rob a helpless victim without unnecessary violence, that decision may represent a great elevation in the area of free choice for him. An action which would be the worst kind of failure for a more elevated person may be a great victory for this person!

On the other hand, consider someone who has reached an elevated state of refinement and self-control, say, a Torah scholar who has toiled for years to understand the depths of Torah and develop his personality. Such an individual is grappling with ordeals so refined that the criminal we considered previously would be entirely unable to relate to them. Perhaps this sage is working to control his speech, to ensure that every word he utters is necessary and true. Or perhaps he is laboring to control his thoughts, one of the most difficult areas to master. This individual is battling in areas which our criminal could not begin to understand.

And if this highly developed person fails in one of his tests, slips from his level of greatness in word or thought, he will yet remain far above the greatest achievement of the criminal. Failure at his elevated level may consist of behavior which would be a supreme achievement for the person at the lower level!

This is known as the point of free will. You are always locked in battle with your lower self, but where the battle is pitched depends on your particular situation and the state of your personal growth.

Your point of free will moves as you make choices. As you handle a free will ordeal, you rise or fall. If you win in your battle with your own lower self, if you overcome your temptation and choose the higher path in your ordeal, you immediately become a higher person. As you exert effort to defeat the temptation, as you push through the test successfully, you rise. Just as physical exertion against resistance builds muscle, so spiritual effort builds spiritual power. As you overcome your own immaturity, you develop your inner being. As you conquer tests, you conquer yourself, you take control and you build yourself.

Your growth is in direct proportion to the effort you exert.

If you lose the battle in an ordeal, you fall, you become a lesser person. And if you fail to engage your ordeals, if you give up without a struggle, you become a lesser person. Just as muscles weaken if they are not constantly stressed, your inner being becomes weaker if you are not straining against resistance and winning.

As you conquer ordeals, you must face more difficult ordeals. As you grow, you are given tests which are more difficult. Just as an athlete must face ever stronger opponents as he develops skill in order for the game to remain a challenge, so must you face ever more difficult tests in order for your free will to remain free. If you grew as a result of a test, but the next test remained as easy as the previous one, *you would immediately outgrow free choice.* When a player outgrows the "little league" it would be pointless (and ridiculous) to continue playing against children. When a club player rises to the level where he can easily defeat all the members of his club, he must go on to play in the national league where he must pit his skill against other champions. There he will find challenge, and there of course, if he exerts himself appropriately, he will develop further. For free choice to remain free, your point of free choice must rise as you rise.

Put another way, your negativity grows along with your positivity. As your positive or spiritual side grows, so does your negative or dark side. Your pull to evil grows in exact proportion to your pull to good. A greater person has *more* temptation than a lesser person. If free will ordeals must remain real ordeals, real challenges, then the individual who is growing and facing new ordeals must experience a more powerful evil in those ordeals exactly as he must experience a more powerful good.

WHY DO ORDEALS BECOME MORE DIFFICULT?

So if you ask *why* your ordeals become more difficult as you grow, why your negativity grows with your positivity, the answer is that you are here to exercise your free will, and the only way to do that throughout life is to be faced with ordeals which are pitched exactly at your level always. As your level goes up, your tests become more difficult, and of course by overcoming a new test at a higher level, you grow further. Your drive to do that which is negative, your drive to harm and destroy, grows *exactly* as much as your higher drive.

Just as the previous ordeal was pitched exactly at the point where your positive and negative drives were locked in a life-and-death struggle for supremacy, so too the new ordeal is pitched at your new point of free choice, both sides of your character are more powerful, and the battle is fought again. But you are greater, the enemy within is more powerful, and the stakes are higher. You are closer to your inner potential, the final victory of life is that much closer, you have become a more worthy opponent of your own darker side, and of course you have further to fall if you fail.

HOW DOES THE POTENTIAL FOR EVIL GROW?

If we ask *how* it is that negativity grows with positivity, how your drive to evil grows as your spiritual refinement increases, we will discover a principle in the world of the spirit. The mechanism of the growth of the darker side of the personality is this:

There are in fact not two separate personalities within you; the opposing sides of your character which are locked in the battle for the real you *are one and the same.* There is only one being within: you. And that single being can be directed in one of two directions, good or evil. And of course, with exactly equal force: the only difference lies in the direction you choose.

This reflects a general rule in the world: there are no intrinsically good or bad things. Things themselves are not good or bad; only *the manner in which they are used* is good or evil. Money is neither good nor bad; it is entirely neutral. The question is: how is that money used? It may be used for equally good or evil purposes. In fact, in exact proportion to the good which can be achieved with money is the evil it can produce. More money means more power, but that power is neutral, it waits to be directed to the good or to the bad. More money can achieve larger benefits, but of course it can achieve more evil to the same degree. *Things are not good or bad, only more or less powerful.*

The electric current supplying your home is enough to power a household of appliances. On the other hand, if you accidentally put your finger into the socket the result is unpleasant and dangerous. But the high tension lines supplying a city carry enough power for the entire city –

much more energy than the current in your home and able to achieve much more. But if you touched one of those lines, you would be fried. More power means more can be done, but the danger increases in proportion to the potential for good.

Money, good looks, charismatic personality, powers of persuasion – all these are neutral. The more one has, the more powerful one is. But not better or worse: that depends on the purposes and ends to which one applies those gifts and talents. And that is your true measure: not how talented you are, *but rather the degree of control that you exert* over your talents. For what purpose do you use your looks, your intelligence? Good or bad? That decision is, in fact, the real you. You are your free choices.

FREE WILL IN ACTION

Let us attempt to put together the elements we have been studying by considering some practical examples. Consider someone who is going through a free will ordeal; it may be a man alone with a woman, or it may be any test of morality or conscience, any situation in which the pleasures of the body, for example, are pitted against the refinement of conscience.

Imagine a person who steps out of his office for lunch. He is about to enter the shellfish restaurant where he usually eats. He is accustomed to eating unkosher food; perhaps he was brought up with inadequate knowledge of the importance of kosher food, perhaps he has moved away from Jewish observance. As he is about to enter, he is struck by the thought that he should really consider what he is about to do. Perhaps there is something to the idea of kosher food, after all. Perhaps he should take it more seriously; perhaps changing to a kosher diet would be the spiritually correct thing to do. He is caught in an ordeal: his higher self is fighting for control, for the elevated choice of self control, of living up to the laws and values of his people. And his lower self craves pleasure, self-indulgence and the easy way of simply doing what feels good.

He stands there, locked in battle with himself. The battle may take quite some time, and it may be surprisingly difficult. He may stand there, sweating and shaking, for long minutes. Let us say he overcomes the desire for his accustomed meal, and decides to enter a kosher delicatessen instead, where he will order food which is not his favorite type of food at all. This individual has achieved victory in a test. His higher self, his higher world of values, has overcome his lower self, his lower world of physical pleasures. He has grown to a new level; he is a new person. He has a measure of self-control which he did not have before, and he has made a move along the road to perfection of character, out of the grip of thoughtless desire.

What happens the next day? Our hero steps out for lunch again, and the same battle occurs: again he is tempted, and again he battles. But the battle is easier, the agony is less. Let us say he overcomes the ordeal. What happens on the third day? If he overcomes his ordeal again, very soon he will be eating a kosher lunch *with no battle at all.* He is now *in the habit* of eating a kosher lunch. He has a new behavior pattern which costs no effort to maintain. *He has outgrown his ordeal in that area of his life.* That which he does out of habit is not at the point of free will; he has passed beyond being tested in that area *and he no longer gains spiritual reward there*. If there is no battle, there is no reward; if there is no exertion there can be no growth.

Of course, we should not become confused: for this individual, the benefits of kosher food still apply, and the harm of eating unkosher food is still avoided. But the special dimension of fighting the battle to acquire that particular *mitzva* as part of his life is no longer active.

And of course, now he will be faced with a new challenge, one which he could not have faced before. He was previously too insensitive, too much in the unthinking grip of his habits at the lower level; now, at his new level of sensitivity he enters the arena of new and more subtle battles. And if he wins at the new level, he grows again, and he will face new battles yet again when this level becomes old habit. Battles are always being fought at the point of free will, and that point is always changing.

A classic image has been used to illustrate this process: your point of free will is like the front line in a war. When two countries are at war, the sharp pain and conflict are felt at the front line. Although each country in its entirety is at war with the entire country of the enemy, the battle is only where they meet. Your higher self is locked in battle with your lower self, the battle is for victory over all that you are, but the conflict is felt only at the point of free will. As one army advances and the other retreats, the front line moves; as your higher self develops and your lower self is brought under control, the area of your free will shifts. And of course the battle can rage in either direction: the enemy can advance into your territory and force you to retreat, you can find yourself losing and sinking. That is exactly what free will means.

The war rages on, and it lasts as long as you live. There are advances today and retreats tomorrow, victories and defeats. Some setbacks are inevitable; you will not win all your battles. But the main thing to keep in focus is steady gain, steady progress towards controlling and mastering the personality. Your aim should be to win as often as possible and to learn from your failures so that even those can be used to build perfection in the long run.

THE ROLE OF EXTERNAL FORCES

What about things that seem to be outside the arena of free choice entirely? What about someone with a significant psychological problem, or an extreme situation which appears to force a person to act in a certain way? What about real disadvantages of upbringing, culture or intelligence? Do we say that such a person is not free? Are they to blame if they fail in a situation in which someone else not suffering from the same disadvantage would have coped? Let us think this through.

Consider someone who feels a deep compulsion to steal. Some time ago a young woman was arrested for stealing candy in a supermarket; this was her tenth arrest for this problem. She is intelligent, attractive and belongs to a wealthy family; in fact she has all the candy she can eat right at home and has enough money to buy more whenever she wishes. However, she feels a surge of overwhelming pleasure when she steals candy in a store. Her psychiatrist must testify before the court that she understands what she is doing and knows that it is wrong and immoral. In fact, she hates herself for it and wishes that she could stop; she is certainly aware that it is wrong. She simply has a craving for this particular behavior which most other people do not.

Now the question is: is she responsible for her actions? Does she have free will in this area of her life? Is she to be blamed? Punished?

The answer is that the *urge* to steal may be presently outside the area of free will for this individual. That is to say: she feels a real urge and has a real craving, and it is quite possible that the origin of the problem is outside her range of freedom; she may be unable to suppress feeling that urge. *But the action of stealing is within her free choice* – she is responsible. As long as she remains in contact with reality, as long as she knows right from wrong, as long as there is no unstoppable force moving her to take the candy, she is free at her point of choice when she reaches out to take that candy bar.

The fact that her ordeal is in the area of stealing candy may be outside her free choice. That is her ordeal for whatever reason has caused the development of her particular craving, whether that reason is genetic or environmental or some combination of factors. It is quite possible that she has not chosen this ordeal, this problem. In other words, her point of free choice is here, at the point of choosing between stealing and not stealing. That may be outside of her doing, and it may be inappropriate to blame her for having such a nature.

But what she does at her point of free choice, whether she steals or not, is her responsibility. Whether she yields to her nature or rises to control it is her test; that is the expression of her free will.

In other words, where your point of free choice begins may be outside your control. You may have an immense urge to do something improper which others may not feel. One person may have a moral ordeal which others may consider no battle at all. Every person has a different point of free will, and within each individual there may be different points of free will in different areas of life. And those points of free will may in fact be set by genetics, upbringing, education, social norms and behavior and many other factors.

But what you do at your point of free will is up to you. Once you are doing battle with your particular ordeal, you are free to win or lose. You may be able to blame others for the fact that you have a particular ordeal, that may be true; but how you cope with that ordeal is your doing entirely.

And of course, you grow or fall depending on how you manage your own ordeals. You are expected to cope only with your own tests, to overcome yourself at your point of free will only. You are never accountable for living up to standards that are not yours, for battling at points of freedom that are not yours. Your task is to win your own battles, to defeat your own inner enemy, not someone else's.

THE MODERN APPROACH

Note how different this approach is from that of the secular world around us. The world thinks that if a person has a particular problem, an urge or a seemingly unfair disadvantage, that person is not accountable for his or her actions. They might look upon our young lady stealing candy as though she were caught in the grip of an unstoppable compulsion, as though she were not free at all; and they would perhaps absolve her of moral responsibility. They may even consider her to be totally controlled by her drive to steal, totally unable to act differently.

And that is not true. That she has a genuine problem is quite true. That we must relate to her with sympathy and understanding, of course. That the origin of her problem may be beyond her free choice and even her understanding, certainly. But that she cannot act differently, that she cannot resist the act of theft if she exerts herself and tries enough – certainly not. She may not have chosen her ordeal, but she certainly chooses her behavior in that ordeal.

You are not responsible for where your point of free choice starts out, only for what you do with it from there on.

Of course, there are situations outside of free will entirely: a child does not have real moral ordeals and is not morally responsible. There are psychiatric states that make free choice impossible. But as long as a mentally competent adult is able to decide and act in a moral ordeal, that person is free, no matter how difficult the correct decision and action may be.

THE TWO VIEWS: A PRACTICAL EXAMPLE

Let us look at one more practical example in order to sharpen our understanding of the difference between the point of free will and the actual choice made at that point. Note again how Judaism approaches these situations, unlike the modern secular trend.

Not long ago, a group of youths from an inner city slum attacked a young woman as she jogged through the park near her home. They brutalized her terribly and left her desperately badly injured, and later admitted that they had done so "for fun".

During their trial, the defense raised was that they came from disadvantaged backgrounds – broken homes, raised by parents with unstable and criminal histories, exposed to violence and poverty. *And therefore they cannot be blamed,* stated the defense; they are guiltless.

Their behavior is nothing other than the inevitable outcome of a problematic childhood, a violent upbringing. How could they be expected to behave otherwise? How could standards appropriate to more privileged members of society be applied to them?

And for the secular court which heard the case, this argument posed a serious challenge. One cannot deny the force of the observation that such behavior may be related to exactly those sociological and societal issues targeted by the defense in this case as being the cause of the crime.

What does Judaism say about this? Are we insensitive to these issues of background and deprivation?

The answer should be clear by now. Of course the disadvantaged and violent background of such individuals is relevant. Of course they are tempted in ways that more refined and sensitive individuals may not be; and that is exactly the point: *their problematic and disturbed backgrounds may be the reason that they found themselves in that ordeal.* A morally trained and finely raised person would not have had that ordeal in the first place; on the contrary, a morally sensitive person would be *nauseated* by the thought of doing what they did, not *tempted* by it.

But that does not mean that they were not free to act differently than they did. The depth of the deprivation and cruelty of their childhoods does not mean that they had become machines, robots, incapable of controlling their violent urges completely. The social problems they had experienced had not made them psychotically detached from reality, mindless animals with no capacity to tell right from wrong entirely. Of course they may have had a real ordeal, of course it may have been difficult, perhaps extremely difficult. Perhaps it would have taken a high degree of self-control for any of those young men to restrain himself from the violence he committed. And the blame for that problem may in fact properly be laid at the doorstep of the violent and uncaring parents who abandoned or mistreated them, or perhaps at the doorstep of a violent and uncaring society. *But as long as they were able to act differently, they are responsible.*

They may not be responsible for the circumstances of their lives or for where those circumstances have led them, they may not be responsible for what appeals to them and tempts them; but where they find themselves tempted and tested, they are responsible for their actions.

Again, the nature and the difficulty of your tests may be beyond your control, out of your hands. But within any test you face, victory or defeat is in your hands.

REWARD AND PUNISHMENT

And of course, this means reward and punishment too. Let us understand this.

When you succeed in an ordeal, the spiritual reward is in proportion to the effort you exert to win that battle. In fact, at a deeper level, that effort is the reward itself, because the effort not only overcomes the test, *it builds you.* You are the achievements you have attained in your tests. *That is all you are.* The starting point of your tests, the raw material you have been given in life to apply in your free will battles, those are not you. Your raw material of intelligence and personality, mind and body, are tools only. What you achieve with that raw material is the real you. And only against resistance.

So when you struggle against a test which is enormously difficult and you overcome it, you gain tremendous reward even though someone else would not have had an ordeal in that situation at all.

When our young lady driven to take candy in a supermarket manages to overcome that urge, she grows tremendously even though you may experience her ordeal as trivial. You may have no urge to take candy that is not yours – and if that is so, *you gain no reward when you succeed.* For you it is not a test; when you stroll along the aisle in your local supermarket you experience no urge to take candy at all. And that is why you earn no reward there, that is not your test. But the young lady whose problem we have been studying gains great reward when she overcomes her urge; that is her problem and that is where she must grow.

You earn no reward when you avoid brutalizing some girl jogging through the park. The very idea would turn your stomach. You need exert no effort to overcome such a temptation, and therefore you gain no reward. But someone else may.

Of course, a human court does not, cannot, measure the effort that may have been required to overcome a particular test. That is a spiritual matter. The human court may have to apply a more uniform standard, and therefore two individuals may receive the same verdict in court for the same crime even though they may have experienced very different inner struggles in committing that crime. But their spiritual growth or fall will be very different; each one's inner reality will have changed in proportion to the difficulty he experienced in dealing with his test.

CONFLICT IN THE SECULAR APPROACH

As we have noted, there is a move in the thinking of Western society, particularly in the fields of psychology, sociology and criminology towards a position which holds that we are not free at all. Much research is devoted to demonstrating that certain behavior patterns are linked to genetic or biochemical factors. Violence, criminal behavior and other behavioral patterns have been linked to particular genetic variations or other biological factors. The trend seems to be towards seeing these factors as so significant that the individuals who possess them are not free; their genetic constitution determines their behavior and it is the cause of their actions.

Taken to its logical extreme, such an attitude would make nothing criminal and nothing punishable; after all, you cannot punish someone for doing that which is his only option, that which his inner nature causes him to do. Humans are increasingly seen as biological creatures acting according to their inner forces with no real free will at all, just as plants and animals act out the results of their biological inputs.

Taking this line of thinking further, it must also logically follow that you cannot reward people for positive moral behavior either. If we are not free to choose our actions, then of course even apparently great and heroic actions must be the result of inner drives and forces too. Speeches of praise and admiration, awarding of medals for bravery and all other forms of recognition of human achievement become absurd – if people are really only biological creatures, animals, then you cannot talk about achievement or failure, about morality or immorality. Just as we see the actions of animals as morally neutral, just as when a gorilla takes a banana away from another gorilla we do not talk about immorality or stealing, and just as when a mother animal risks her life to save her cubs we do not talk about heroism and idealism but only about instincts, so too if we are to be consistent we should speak of human actions in the same terms.

If you accept that we are animals, then it follows that we act out our biological instincts and inner forces just as animals do.

Judaism rejects this position entirely.

Judaism's position should be clear after our discussion of free choice and the point of free choice: our understanding is that when you are placed in an ordeal, you are free to choose your response. What you do is up to you. *You* are in control; you decide and you act.

Do not ask why someone responded in a particular way in a test; the answer is that they acted that way *because they chose to.* Do not say that they acted as they did *because* of their genes or their upbringing; those things explain only why the person experienced the ordeal and why it was as difficult as it was. Genes and upbringing and all the other factors which may affect us and our ordeals affect an individual's point of free will in an ordeal, but they do not *cause* that individual's action. In the entire world outside of the human being, the inputs cause the output. Plants and animals do what they do because that is what their inputs determine. But in people, the inputs cause the ordeals, not the responses. *We* are the cause of our actions in the free will arena.

THE REAL YOU

What you do in your tests is who you are. Your choices are the reflection of your character. That is where you reveal your level, that is where your real achievement lies. Real success or failure is success or failure in your free will ordeals.

Making life decisions and acting on them is the deepest expression of yourself. When you choose and act, you are expressing that part of your inner being *that has no prior cause;* it is the root. When you grasp the fact that you are in control, that where it really matters you are free, you have begun to grasp who you really are and what you are meant to be doing here.

As long as you see your decisions and actions as the passive results of your background and your nature, beyond your control and outside your ability to change and master, you have not begun to live.

Choose and live. Choose the correct options in your tests; choose to live correctly. Choose and elevate your point of free will with every choice; choose and grow. Express your real depth and choose wisely and courageously. Choose and live.

Chapter 2

Happiness

Happiness. It is probably the focus and goal of most societies on earth. In the popular culture of the West, happiness is set up as the ultimate achievement. A very large part of human striving is aimed at achieving happiness and the means to secure it. People long to be happy.

QUESTIONS

What is the Jewish view of this subject? Are we meant to be happy? Are we meant to strive for happiness? Is happiness a Jewish goal? Is it a *mitzva*, a commandment? What is the path that leads to happiness in a world of ordeals?

And is it possible to achieve happiness in a sad world? How can you be happy while you know that there are people suffering – do you forget them long enough to have a good time? Should you really forget their pain so that you can enjoy yourself? And how are those individuals who suffer meant to rise above their suffering and be happy? Is that possible? Let us analyze this subject.

Firstly, is it a *mitzva* to be happy? There is no direct commandment to be happy; it is not one of the 613 formal commandments of the Torah. And yet we find statements in the Torah and in the words of the Sages to the effect that we should be happy. Why? What sort of obligation is this? Why is it not expressed as a commandment if it is worth striving for?

"Serve Hashem ("the Name" of God) with joy." Here it would seem that we are obliged to be happy; the verse states thus. Again, what is the nature of this obligation?

Also, when the Torah describes the horrific curses which will befall the Jewish people if we fail to live up to our Torah obligations, after listing the most agonizing holocaust-type brutalities which we will suffer, it states the reason for these horrors: "Because you did not serve Hashem your God with joy..." It appears, almost incredibly, that the reason for our immense suffering throughout history is that we failed to be joyous – is this possible? Is it even conceivable? Is *that* the problem – lack of joy?

And anyway, how can you be happy in a world full of suffering without becoming tremendously insensitive to that suffering? How many people do you have to know who are suffering intensely before it affects *your* ability to be happy?

Surely, if you are aware of even one person who is in pain you should be unable to rejoice. How can you be aware of an individual's suffering and have a good time? And if you manage to be happy by forgetting that individual, surely that is tremendous insensitivity? Yet how can you be happy if you do *not* forget – surely rejoicing while you are aware of someone's pain is even more insensitive?

The world's approach to this problem is simply to forget, to become unaware, to block out the awareness of human suffering and sadness and to have a good time anyway.

But that is not Judaism. Judaism requires and develops awareness, not forgetfulness. We do not forget that the world is full of pain; we do not forget those who suffer.

How then do we achieve happiness?

Even more difficult is the question of happiness for those very people who are suffering. How do you put aside your own pain and achieve happiness? Is it possible? The Torah sources that speak about the obligation to be happy do not distinguish between people who are comfortable and those who are in pain. It seems that *everyone* is required to be happy – what does this mean and how is it to be done?

And seemingly impossible to understand, Torah sources suggest clearly that *everyone* should be happy *always* – surely this is downright impossible? What about the *mitzva* of mourning, for example? How on earth can one be happy in the face of a situation which demands the response of mourning?

The great Chazon Ish, Torah leader of the previous generation, makes a statement in one of his letters which seems so extreme that it appears impossible to understand. Loosely translated, he states: "For one who knows the light of truth, there is no sadness in the world." No sadness in the world? How can anyone make such an assertion? The Chazon Ish himself lived through the agony of the Second World War; he had his own personal tragedies. How can a man say such things?

THE ANSWER

The answer to these questions is one of the most important secrets of life; understanding it well can make the difference between a life of frustration, even depression, and success. Very few subjects are as critical to self-fulfillment as this.

The answer depends on understanding correctly what happiness is:

Real happiness is what you experience when you are doing what you should be doing.

When you are moving clearly along your own road, your unique path to your unique destination, you experience real happiness. When you are moving along the path that leads to *yourself,* to the deep discovery of who you really are; when you are building the essence of your own personality and *creating yourself,* a deep happiness wells up within you. The journey does not cause happiness – *the journey is the happiness itself.*

And amazingly, the expression on your face may not be a smile. The face may reflect pain, the face may be tearstained and taut with strain; but if the journey is proceeding, if you are aware that you are building what you must build, your heart will be singing within you despite the pain of your body and the tears on your face.

And even more amazingly, your heart will be singing *because of the pain.* This needs explanation; let us think into it carefully.

The truth is that the journey of life is always made against resistance. Life is work, and work is always performed against resistance. When you strain against the resistance of ordeals and difficulties and move ahead, when you perceive that you are winning the battle and moving, building, your deepest essence experiences happiness even while your body is aching. And that happiness is generated by the experience of moving ahead against resistance, building when the building is difficult. Things that come easy give only a superficial happiness; if no work is invested there can be very little satisfaction.

One or two practical examples will make this idea clear.

Imagine you are carrying rocks and heavy logs and assembling them in the heat of the day. You are building something important and you have limited time. You sweat and shake with effort as you labor to complete your task, working against time and the limits of your physical abilities.

What do you experience as you see the result taking shape? What emotion fills you as you realize that you will complete your task in time? What deep and rich feeling swells within despite your raw hands, shaking limbs and grime-streaked face, despite the gasps of exertion and the tears of pain and effort?

There is no doubt that the inner experience is happiness. The fact that the outer expression is one of pain is irrelevant; on the contrary, if the pain is a measure of your effort, if the pain is felt because you are giving all to do what you must do, that pain is the cause of the joy. In fact, it is the joy itself.

Words are inadequate to express the depth of what is happening here, but if you have ever really struggled and suffered to build, you will know exactly what is meant.

And if you have never struggled and suffered to build anything, you have not lived.

Consider another illustration.

Imagine a newcomer to civilized society. He is taken on a tour of mankind's activities. Let us suppose that the first place our visitor inspects is a modern gymnasium, one of those establishments in which people exercise on machines and lift weights. Let us say that our visitor peeps through the keyhole and witnesses a young man exercising on a machine or lifting extremely heavy weights. On the young man's face is an expression of agony; sweat is pouring from him and he appears close to the limit of human endurance. His body is racked by tremors of exertion as he strains to lift weights at the very limits of his ability.

There can be little doubt that our visitor would conclude that our young man is being tortured. He would immediately decide that just beyond his range of vision there must stand a menacing aggressor with a weapon trained on this unfortunate victim who is being cruelly worked to exhaustion.

But the truth is that the young man is working voluntarily. No-one is forcing him. In fact, he is *paying* for the privilege of being able to work thus. And most important of all: *he is loving every moment!* And anyone who has ever engaged in that sort of effort knows that *the pain is the pleasure.*

The pain is the pleasure because it is the pain that is building what he wants to build. If that young man wants to build muscle, he knows that it is the effort that builds that muscle. The pain is the measure of the effort; the pain is the exact measure of how much is being built. Without the pain, there can be no building. Without the straining against resistance there can be no progress. As they say in those circles which deal with such things: "No pain, no gain." True.

THE JOURNEY AND THE DESTINATION

Let us go further. The pain itself is pleasurable because it is the means of building the desired result; but there is more. The depth of the pleasure felt in the intensity of the effort is really the anticipation of the result. It is the looking forward to what is being built; the vision of the end-point, that fuels the effort. The dream of the satisfaction of achieving the result provides the pleasure within the pain of the journey. *The more one looks forward to the joy of the end-point the more one enjoys the labor of getting there.*

You can see this clearly by considering its opposite: imagine you are forced to labor intensely on something which is to be destroyed before it is completed – that would be torture. If you knew that your effort would achieve no result at all, that effort would become sheer pain. The sweetness of the journey lies in the anticipation of reaching the destination. In every bit of effort, in every moment of exertion, lies the awareness that a part of the result has been built, and that is its happiness. In fact, in many experiences in life, the anticipation is more pleasurable than the result itself.

So the work derives its happiness from the expectation of the end-point.

And amazingly, the end-point derives its happiness from the work! If you think about it deeply, you will realize that the real satisfaction of the result lies in the fact that your work built it! A result which happens without effort, a gift received free, means far less than a result which you labored to achieve. The depth of your happiness at the journey's end lies in the effort that you invested to get there. The rich satisfaction you feel when you look at what you have built is really the knowledge of how hard you worked to build it. The delicious taste of a hard-won result derives almost entirely from the knowledge of how hard you worked to get there. In fact, *the result is you because you invested yourself to create it.*

DEEP ROOTS

Why is all this so? Why is the world built this way in the first place? What can we learn about the nature of the world from this understanding of the relationship between work and result, journey and destination?

Life is a journey through the world. And the next world is the destination. The Torah concept is that life is movement, a journey to a destination. The next world is the destination of that journey, and the journey has meaning only because there is a destination.

If you grasp your life as a journey to an amazing destination, the building of an eternal result, the difficulties of life become meaningful. *In fact, it is those very difficulties which build the result most significantly.*

And our idea of that result is that it is pure pleasure. The Jewish idea of the next world is that it is a dimension of pleasure, and the pleasure is exactly the feeling, the knowledge, that you built it.

Our concept of the next world is that it is a state in which you experience yourself absolutely clearly. No illusions, no facades. Just you. If you have built yourself correctly, achieved your potential through the hard work of a life lived to the full, the result is the ecstasy of being exactly what you should be and knowing that you are the cause of your own achievement. Nothing could bring a deeper happiness.

(And the opposite: our concept of the pain of the next world is the experience, the knowledge, that you could have achieved greatness and failed. If the opportunity of life has been wasted, the pain is immense. And it is nothing other than the pain of a self which might have been, should have been, and was not.)

Life is temporary, but the result is eternal. The work of life may be painful, but it builds a result which is pure happiness and that happiness is forever. In other words, the limited, finite dimension of this world and its effort creates an unlimited dimension of happiness.

And that is why any work in the world which produces a result contains the potential for a feeling of joy: it is a small sample of the joy of life itself.

Since everything in this world is a reflection of the larger reality that creates it, every experience in the world contains a spark of that larger reality. Any experience of building and enjoying the result of that building contains within it the spark of the process of life itself and the joy of translating the limited into the infinite.

The reason that we feel a surge of joy when we build something, achieve something, in this world is because in every small achievement in this world lies the seed of eternity, a reflection of the eternal achievement of a lifetime of work. The energy underlying our experience of any achievement is the same energy that builds the process of translating this world into the next. In every small achievement, every small experience of transforming sweat and effort into a hard-won result, lies the exhilaration of the ultimate achievement of transforming all of life and its effort into an eternal result.

That is why the pleasure felt in the work itself derives from the anticipation of the result, and the pleasure of the result derives from the satisfaction of the hard work done to get there – that is exactly the pattern of life itself: the work of life itself draws inspiration from the knowledge that every moment of difficulty here will live forever in the next world, and the pleasure of the next world is nothing other than all the moments of exertion of the life which built it.

In fact, every pleasure you experience in life derives from nothing less than your future in the next world – that is the essence and nature of pleasure. The sensation of pleasure has a very high source indeed.

BACK TO THE BEGINNING

Now we can begin to understand the answer to the questions we posed at the beginning of our discussion:

"Serve Hashem with joy." Does this mean that there is an obligation to try to be happy? Is it a *mitzva* to be happy? Is happiness an end in itself? The verse is clear: it does not state "Be happy"; that is not the aim. It states *"Serve* Hashem with happiness"; that is the aim. That is the emphasis: serving, working to build, that is the primary obligation; and in that serving the proper mode is joy. If you serve as you should, the joy is guaranteed. If you take care of the work, the happiness will take care of itself.

And "Because you did not serve Hashem your God with joy..." The reason for our suffering throughout history is not that we failed to be joyous – that is not the problem. The problem is not that part of the verse; it is the *beginning* of the verse, that is the key: "Because you did not *serve."* Defaulting on the service, the work that is required of us, that is the problem. And of course, as we have explained, if there is no work, there is no joy.

Happiness is not the goal, but it is *the assured result* of moving towards the goal.

For one who knows this secret deeply and lives it, for one who is always moving towards the goal, indeed "there is no sadness in the world."

DEPRESSION

With this knowledge we can begin to understand a most important and painful subject: depression. What is the cause of depression? Depression is one of the major problems of our age. The ideas we have studied will give us an insight into this area.

A central feature of the sensation of depression is the feeling of hopelessness and despair, the feeling of no movement towards any goal, the feeling of the impossibility of reaching any goal. And the cause of depression is exactly that: *absence of movement towards a goal.* When the *neshama,* the soul, senses that life is sliding by and no meaningful progress is taking place, no real development is occurring, there is a sense of stagnation, of despair. Happiness is the response of the *neshama* to its journey through life, the response of the *neshama* to its own development, its own growth and achievement. And depression is the response of the *neshama* to stagnation, to a situation of motionlessness and the absence of achievement.

Your *neshama* knows that it is here to grow, to develop. That journey is the essence of life. So when your *neshama* senses that the journey has come to a halt, that life is sliding by and you are going nowhere, you will become depressed. The journey is life itself, every step on that journey is essential and priceless (you cannot get to your destination unless you walk the *entire* road that leads there), and therefore when time is passing but the journey is not progressing the *neshama* feels the cold hand of death. Depression is no less than a minor experience of death itself; that is exactly why it is so painful.

A depressed person may not know that this is the cause of the problem, but the soul knows. It is weeping, crying out to be allowed to move on, to move actively and urgently to its destination, and it is being obstructed. It is being held back from the most urgent and important task that there is, the task of building itself and its eternity in a race against time. If it fails to build itself now it will exist forever incomplete, deeply lacking. That would be disastrous, painful beyond description. So the response of the soul is a feeling of deep pain, of life and its opportunity lost. And it is possibly the deepest pain there is.

The problem of organic (or medical) states of depression is outside the scope of this discussion. Here we are referring to the depression experienced by people who have not yet discovered their unique path in life, those whose lives seem pointless because there is no real work being done, no meaningful exertion being expended in a positive direction.

What is the cure for depression? What should we tell someone who is depressed? What does such a person need to do?

The answer is: get moving! If the problem is lack of meaningful movement, *get busy moving* in the right direction. As soon as the soul feels that it is moving and on the correct course for its own development and fulfillment, it will forget all sadness; the depression will end. *You cannot feel depressed when you know you are moving correctly towards a correct goal.*

You may feel pain, you may feel agony; your face may show strain and your eyes may fill with tears, but if you are winning the battle and moving ahead you cannot be depressed.

Sometimes it is necessary to start the movement in an external area: getting the body moving may be necessary before the soul can be roused. Judaism teaches that the "external awakens the internal"; experiences and actions of the body will stimulate experience of the soul. It may be necessary to begin with physical exercise or occupation for the hands so that the outer can begin to drive inward and affect the soul. But the idea remains: cure stagnation with movement, passive wallowing in misery with activity.

You cannot approach someone who is depressed and say: "Be happy." That will not work. Instead, take that person for a run, get them moving, doing. Best of all, get them busy doing something for someone else.

And the real cure will be felt when the soul gets moving, when the personality begins its unique journey towards its unique destination.

One who is laboring to achieve, to build, and is aware that the result is taking shape as it should *cannot be depressed* no matter how hard the work.

SELF-ESTEEM

A major problem for many of today's youth (and adults) is low self-esteem. A healthy self-esteem requires *knowing who you are, knowing what you must become, and knowing that you are getting there.* If you know yourself, if you have a clear vision of your goal, and if you are feeling genuine movement towards that goal, your self-esteem will be intact. Not just intact; it will be throbbing and vital. When you know that you are fulfilling your potential and becoming the very best you can be, you will have such a rich sense of self-worth that you will glow with confidence and positivity.

(Of course, you need to know yourself and discover what your unique goal should be; we shall study this later in our discussion on "Who Are You? Defining Your Role in Life", the subject of Chapter 5.)

But if you are not moving, if you are vague and unsure about where you should be going and you have no sense of your own development, you will certainly lack self-esteem. You cannot have esteem for yourself if you do not know who you are. If you are going around in circles in the confused search for yourself, your self-esteem will be spiraling down too. *Self-esteem is the automatic result of a sharp, clear focus on your unique personality and the perception that your uniqueness is being fulfilled.* If you are not working hard on these things, your deepest sense of self will stagnate and dissolve.

TRAVELLING THE WRONG ROAD

There is another way to avoid depression and the pain of non-growth: the wrong way.

It is possible to satisfy the deep need to build and achieve by building and achieving trivial things; to channel the drive to build into superficial areas. This escape often provides a sense of achievement, a sense of work transformed into result, which is *enough to keep a person from the real task* of working on the self without the warning signs of a feeling of emptiness or depression.

People will build collections of objects or throw themselves into projects which are meaningless because this gives them a sense of purpose and movement; the fact that the purpose is irrelevant or foolish is ignored.

Some people build collections of beer cans, some build collections of valuable paintings. Some devote themselves to sporting achievement, some to business. Some people build muscle, some build empires. All of these have the potential to satisfy the need to produce, to move, to build, at least for a while.

But very often they are simply the superficial substitute for the really hard work of building the self.

There is nothing wrong with building things in this world; some of those things may be necessary and most worthy. But when the building here becomes a substitute for the real work of building the self, building that which will last for eternity, that is a tragedy. This world and its achievements must always be the vehicle for the real journey.

You cannot afford to forget that the road leads somewhere; you cannot afford to forget the destination. Consider this:

A man hired a truck driver to deliver a load of goods to a distant city. "Drive carefully," he instructed the driver. "Take good care of the truck, obey all the rules of the road, do not do anything dangerous. Do not speed, take no chances."

Two days later, the driver was back. "How did it go?" asked the man who had hired him.

"Fine," said the driver, "I did exactly as you instructed. I took care of the truck, I obeyed all the rules of the road, I drove safely all the way and I took no chances."

"Did you deliver the goods as arranged?"

"Oh!" said the driver, "I forgot to deliver the goods!"

You cannot afford to forget to deliver the goods. Do not get so involved in the journey that you forget where you are going. Do not get so involved in the excitement of doing and moving and building that you forget to ask yourself where it all leads. You do not want to travel for years and then discover that it has been the wrong road, or that you were so preoccupied with the trivia of the journey that you hardly moved at all, or that you forgot that you had goods to deliver.

You have goods to deliver: yourself. You have the most important and precious goods to deliver; and only you can deliver them. You have yourself and the future of the Jewish people in your hands, and one day you will be asked that final and most profound question: "Did you deliver the goods?"

DRUGS AND OTHER QUICK FIXES

In modern society, patience has little value – the goal is quick results, quick fixes. The long, hard path is avoided at all costs. Consumer commodities must be ultra-quick, "instant" and "ready-to-eat", computers must perform millions of functions in microseconds or they are "slow", entertainment must provide instant pleasure with no effort, and it is no surprise that relationships are also instant "quick fixes" and instantly disposable.

And of course, drugs are a massive problem in our generation. The reason is not hard to find: a culture that seeks pleasure and avoids long, hard work is grasping for exactly those things that provide instant pleasure with no effort. The mindset of seeking instant gratification is a mindset that seeks drugs. We are living in an addicted generation.

Drugs can provide instant pleasure. *And drugs will dissolve your sense of self until you have no personality left.* The pleasure they provide is hollow: it comes from outside of yourself, outside of the dimension of genuine pleasure which is the pleasure of discovering and building yourself. Quick fixes never work; they are indeed quick – quick to come, quicker to leave, and certain to leave you feeling more desperately empty than before.

Every superficial quick fix cheapens you, depresses you, and damages your self-esteem. Every superficial quick fix prostitutes your deeper self, sells out your deeper potential, and in a very deep sense, kills you.

REAL VALUES

And so it is no wonder that depression is widespread and self-esteem is hard to find. Where there is no real work and no real growth, there is sure to be depression and no sense of self-worth. There is depression *because* there is no growth, and there is a lack of self-esteem *because* there is an absence of production of self. Where there is hard work and genuine growth, there is deep happiness and a rich sense of self.

We need the courage to define our own real values, not unthinkingly accept those of the culture we inhabit. The pursuit of happiness as an end in itself, happiness without hard work and a life of quick fixes may seem the proper pursuit of nations and cultures, but it is not ours.

Secular culture wants the happiness of the next world right here in this world, and they want it free. They are willing to sell the self for cheap thrills, to sell deep love for superficial fun, to sell the real pleasure of giving for the immediate gratification of taking and to sell life itself for empty laughs.

That is not Judaism. If you want happiness, you must work for it. If you want to discover yourself and build your self-esteem, you must fight for it.

The road may be long, and it may be difficult. The load may be heavy. But if it is the right road, and you are moving steadily along it, you will understand the real meaning of happiness. Keep moving, keep fighting, keep your eyes on the goal and deliver the goods.

Chapter 3

Man and Woman

Relationships. Man and woman. What makes this aspect of life so dominant, so powerful? Why is the culture around us so preoccupied with this subject? What is its true power and what is its place in Judaism?

What is the nature of the intimacy here and why does it occupy such a prominent part of the human psyche? Why is so much of society's activity and consciousness focused on this aspect of human functioning?

The natural attraction of this area is not due to the drive for pleasure alone – there are many pleasures of the body, yet we do not find society obsessed with any of them in a way even vaguely comparable with its obsession with this subject. The libraries of the world are filled with books which relate to it in one way or another, and a cursory look at the world of advertising will show that virtually everything which can tempt man is promoted by being linked to the temptation of the male-female relationship. That is the center; all else is secondary. Why must this be so?

In this area lie some of the deepest secrets of the world.

If you wish to understand the depth of this subject, you must study and understand the experience of male and female interaction sensitively and accurately. What exactly is the nature of this most potent and fascinating human experience? What does it contain that so captivates the mind and heart? Why does it exert so powerful an attraction that many students of human nature claim that it is the central element in all human motivation?

The answer is that in the intimate depth of this relationship is contained a sensation of end-point, of having arrived, of having no place else to go and in fact no need to go anywhere else at all. The sensation which is generated here is that a process has reached its goal; all movement finally stops here, comes to rest in the deepest sense possible. The pleasure which can be felt here is not simply that of the physical, of nerve endings and animal experience; these elements are immeasurably amplified by a consciousness of end-point, of purpose achieved, of coming home most intensely. This is not a function perceived as process or preparation, it is not fulfilled with a sense of future; rather, past and future melt away in a present so intense that it seems to swell to infinite proportions.

Why is this so? What cosmic energy underlies this interaction? The answer is that here lies the microcosm, the human-sized experience of all purpose achieved, of worlds coming together, of process meeting result, of body and soul joining at root, of life itself. Here lies the sensation of transition from this world to the next, where all process becomes result, where all the pain of work and waiting gives way to the exhilaration of unity with the source.

All that we studied in our discussion on happiness is focused here. Here is contained the ultimate moment of transition from work to result, from journey to arriving at the destination.

Is it any wonder that this area, when sensitively and spiritually entered, has the power to build a depth of relationship which is indescribable, and is it any wonder that this is where life is generated?

And is it any wonder that a non-spiritual generation damages this area above all else? If the animal is loosed in this sacred zone, if human depth and sublime understanding are eliminated from this fragile zone of wonder, if the unique privacy and modesty which belong here are damaged, then there is no spiritual in the world of flesh and there can be no possibility of elevating the physical.

In the battle to be truly human, in the quest for a higher path within the world, this is the fulcrum; here the battle is pitched. The alternatives are clear and compelling – the abandon of animal instinct which senses only the present, or that deep and private sense of investment in a relationship built for eternity.

Let us probe more deeply into this mystery: what is the meaning of the potency of human experience compressed into this area? Why is there this sense of timelessness and ultimate "having arrived" inherent in this particular interaction?

The secret here is startling in its depth: the source of all that is contained in the intimacy between man and woman in this world is in fact the nature of existence in the world to come. The ecstasy of the next world, clumsy though our grasp of it may be, is the bond between the clarified and elevated human soul and the Creator. In that great relationship is contained the ultimate sensation, the knowledge, of having arrived. In that state of togetherness, ultimately and absolutely, there is no other place to go. There, in the deepest sense possible, time and motion stretch into the infinite meshing of the soul with its Source at a cosmic intensity. There, two become One in essence. And there, in the most fundamental sense, life is conceived.

All experience in this world reflects its source in the higher experience. When that higher experience is the ultimate and eternal relationship between the Creator and the human soul, the parallel experience in this world which it generates must be exceptionally potent and ecstatic.

Let us go deeper. A central feature of the soul's experience in the next world is the lack of obligation. This world is built for work, but the essence of the dimension which we call the next world is entirely reward. In that blissful state there is no work to be done; only the fruits of a lifetime's work to be enjoyed.

The sensation is that of being exempt from all work and all obligation. The experience is of ultimate freedom. In fact, when a person leaves this world, the expression we use for that transition indicates exactly the change from work to reward: we say the person is *niftar* – literally "exempt", free of all commandments and obligations.

In this world, the parallel to that ultimate experience of being exempt is the freedom you feel at those moments of being freed of responsibility, those moments of ending a phase of work or obligation. The heady sense of freedom enjoyed at the start of a vacation, at the moment when the doors of the workplace are closed and locked; at the moment when the final school-bell rings and the unfettered weekend beckons; when you stretch out on a beach with no appointments to keep and no responsibilities to fulfill; these are microcosms of the experience of a state in which existence is justified in its own terms, in fact needs no justification at all. These are moments of existence during which time seems to halt, moments during which you feel richly that you are not travelling but that you have arrived.

And the moments during which the feeling of having arrived at a destination from which further movement is irrelevant, impossible, most intensely are those moments during which man and woman find each other most intensely. There, the experience is of life itself.

And therein lies the danger of this zone of intensity: if it is used responsibly, loyally, used only with the intention to build, to sanctify, to bond in a relationship of pure obligation, then it is truly justified. Paradoxically, this experience of freedom must be used in bondage; bondage to a spouse, bondage to purpose and elevation. If this experience is used as an escape from the world of building, from the world of work, then it is entirely out of place because this world is not meant for freedom from growth and obligation; that is the province of the world to come and it cannot be entered here. One who seeks to be free here, to be exempt here, must forfeit the achievements which this world is designed to build.

The Jew does not seek escape or exemption. The sweetness of this world and all its experiences lies in savoring that foretaste of the freedom of the next world *in the very acts of fulfilling obligations* in this world; in truth, those acts are the stuff of eternal freedom. When performed in loyalty, in deep commitment to the deepest purpose, those acts of bondage are acts of building freedom and they resonate with the sensation of real and lasting freedom.

In human experience there is another activity which provides a rich sense of that which is done entirely for its own sake, and that is the unique activity that we call a game. A game is essentially an activity which is enjoyed simply for the sake of the enjoyment it provides. Of course games may be played for a variety of purposes, but if you examine this subject carefully you will find that at the heart of the experience of play lies the pleasure of an activity that leads nowhere; a pure game is played *for no purpose outside of the game itself.* And that is the secret of the pleasure inherent in a game: while I am engrossed in this game, regardless of the specific nature of the game, I am divorced from the world of my obligations; I am in a state of being in which my goal lies within the activity itself, I am not striving towards a point in the future, I am not looking beyond the present at all.

A game may consist of *entirely trivial actions and processes* and yet be a delicious experience – surely this is a strange phenomenon? But on the contrary, that is exactly the secret: because there is nothing inherently meaningful in the moves and actions of the game, there precisely lies its escape. Within a game is a zone of wonder, a zone isolated from the bonds and pressures of the reality of a life which is entirely obligation and work; but the point to grasp is that this isolation from the world of work is not a simple escape of forgetfulness or unconsciousness – it is the nature of a game itself which holds that escape.

If one understands this idea well it will be no surprise to discover that in the deeper sources the higher world is described as a world of play. The Talmud states that Hashem "plays" with the Torah. This sounds strange in the extreme; but if one remembers that Torah *always* deals with essence and *never* with the superficial, one will begin to understand: "playing" in essence means *doing that which is an end in itself*, that which needs no justification outside of itself, that which leads nowhere other than to its own center. Torah is the core and essence of existence, in depth it does not lead outwards, rather, all else leads to it. The world was created for Torah, it is the end-point and Hashem's original and deepest purpose, and therefore His relationship with Torah *must* be described in terms of ultimate *tachlis*, ultimate purpose. He is not using the Torah for a purpose outside of itself, so to speak, but rather all of existence finds its meaning entirely within Torah.

Nothing could be clearer than the meaning of the word itself: in Hebrew, the word for "play" is *sha'ashua*. This is a fascinating word: it is comprised of two similar components, the root *sha* duplicated. This root means "to turn towards" (*"Va'yisha* – And He turned towards..."; and *"lo sha'a* – He did not turn towards...") The double expression of this root in the word *sha'ashua* means quite literally "turning towards the turning towards"! Is this not exactly the idea of a game – the idea of movement towards and within itself entirely?

And that is the source of the happiness and the laughter generated by play in the lower world of human action. The Hebrew words for "laughter" and for "play" are closely related – *tz'chok* and *s'chok*; and it should be no surprise at all that the word used for intimacy between man and wife in Torah is this very word: "And Isaac was causing Rebecca his wife to laugh", referring to marital intimacy. There are no empty expressions in Torah; the delicate and pure language of Torah is always exact.

The next world can be considered as the ultimate experience of play; the ecstasy of pure existence in and of itself. And the intimate bond between Hashem and the human soul in that world is well described in the same terms. The sweetness of pure intimacy, intimacy which includes spirituality, is the sweetness of producing pure fruit in the most real sense.

And it is precisely because real fruit is produced in this area, and therefore because the world depends on this area for the generation of human life itself, that the Creator has invested it with such sweetness – He has spread His honey thickest here as both a revelation of secret depth and as motivation.

One of the great Torah sages of the previous generation used to say that here the honey is thick because here the purpose is most important – the analogy he would give is that of the mother who smears honey on bread so that her child will eat. The mother is more interested in the bread than the honey – she wants the child to eat bread, so she is prepared to make it attractive with honey. The child, however, is interested in the honey – bread alone would not tempt him – and he is prepared to eat the bread in order to taste the honey.

Hashem gives us the sweetness of honey here because He is interested in the real fruits of the male-female relationship – the bringing down of souls into the world, and the love and loyalty which should be built in human marriage. When the bread is coated with honey, it is sweet and the purpose is achieved.

But a bad child *licks off the honey and discards the bread.* A generation which defeats the purpose of this most sacred and purposefully designed area of human functioning, seeking to enjoy its honey while rejecting its responsibility, is no better (and perhaps a lot worse) than an immature child who throws his mother's kindness and wisdom back in her face.

Honey eaten alone is sweet only for a while; it soon becomes unbearable. Tampering with the sweetest dimension of the human experience in a selfish attempt to strip it of its wholesome purpose must lead to destruction; first, destruction of itself, and later, destruction of the fabric of self, family and society.

The Torah prescription is simply to eat the bread with the honey. Escape from obligation, escape from the deep and correct relationship which should exist between man and woman, is escape from the spiritual. The Jew's pathway is clear: to take that experience which naturally takes one out of obligation and *to use it entirely in obligation.* It is to take the function of escape from obligation, of free and unbonded abandon, and to harness exactly that function to the deepest obligation possible. That is the root of our concept of the loyalty that must exist between husband and wife. That is the root of real love, and that is the root of the love that has been the motivation of the Jewish people for using this most important of human experiences to bond ourselves in an eternal continuity through history and beyond.

Chapter 4

Individuality

Y ou are absolutely unique. Unless you discover and build your special uniqueness, you cannot achieve your life's purpose. Let us study the idea of your uniqueness and attempt to define the path that leads to it.

In order to do this we must understand something deep about the structure and organization of the world. The world is exquisitely ordered; the very fact that it can be studied mathematically and scientifically is due to this order.

We can identify three levels of order in the world:

LEVEL I: ORDER ITSELF

The first, "order for the sake of order", is the symmetry and harmony apparent in the world. Our minds, too, are capable of disciplined order – in fact, it is because our minds reflect the order of the universe that we can perceive its ordered nature.

There is a fascinating resonance to these inner and outer patterns of order: when you are in harmony with the world around you, you perceive the harmonious dance of your mind within the world; when you are in disharmony with your surroundings, you perceive the friction between yourself and your environment.

When you are in a situation where order or symmetry is apparent, your response to that symmetry depends on your own inner sense of order or lack of it. For example, if you are travelling by train, what is your response to the symmetrical rhythm of the wheels on the tracks – *clickety-click, clickety-click, clickety-click?* Your response to that rhythm *depends on your own inner rhythm at the time:* if you are at peace, inwardly tranquil, as you may be when travelling towards some pleasantly anticipated destination, the sound is soothing, pleasant, even musical. The inner symmetry and the outer symmetry are resonating in harmony. But if you are in distress inwardly, perhaps travelling to some unpleasant or feared destination, and your thoughts and emotions are in turmoil, *the sound is unbearable.* The outer harmony is mocking your inner disharmony, and you feel the pain of that mockery.

If a man enters his home in a fine, serene mood after a productive, uncomplicated day and notices one item of furniture slightly out of place – one of the chairs around the table not quite in line with the others – he may walk over and adjust it so that everything is perfect. His inner order seeks to be mirrored in the outer world. But if the same individual enters his home at the end of a frustrating, disastrous day and finds everything just as it should be – all the chairs perfectly in line – he may storm over and kick them into total disarray. The perfect symmetry of his environment mocks the disorder within his mind and the result is an angry attempt to reduce all order into chaos. Of course, it is not only furniture which may be angrily treated at such times – all too often it is people: usually those who are closest and deserve it least. A disharmonious relationship with yourself seeks to spill over into disharmonious relationships with others.

A fractured inner world reflects itself in outer breakdown; a healthy inner world reflects itself in outer order. When Rabbi Simcha Zissel, a master of *mussar* (Jewish character-building), would visit his son in yeshiva, he would enter the boy's dormitory room and note the state of the room. If his son's shoes were neatly together under the bed, he would leave without seeing him. He knew that if his son's possessions were neat and organized, so was his mind; there was no need to disturb his studies!

LEVEL II: ORDER FOR RESULTS

The second level of order, "order for the sake of its results", is that type of order in which parts are arranged in such a way that they function. The purpose of the organization of the components is to maintain the proper relationship between them so that each can fulfill its function correctly. An example of this kind of order is a library which is indexed.

The index contains the order of the library; it makes each book accessible. The index is the key to the successful functioning of the library: without it, the library may be useless. The system requires that all the books be arranged correctly and that the index reflects their arrangement.

One feature of this type of order is this: if a library has an index, the more books it contains, the better; however, when the index is lacking, the more books the library contains, the worse! Without an index to enable you to find a particular book, the sheer number of books becomes the problem.

A collection of twenty books will be useful even if its index is disorganized or does not exist: you will find the book you need anyway. But a library of twenty thousand books will be almost useless if its index is disorganized – you will probably never find what you need. You would have been better off with far fewer books.

And thus it is with the order in your mind: the more organized the mind, the more useful are many facts. But the undisciplined, disorganized mind is better off with fewer facts – they are more likely to be accessible in their disarray when they are few in number. One who wishes to know much must first develop structured and orderly thinking.

In fact, the first purpose of Torah learning is to train and discipline the mind. Learning facts is not nearly as important as learning how to discover those facts; real wisdom is knowing how to think, not simply knowing a lot of information. Your first goal in all your studies should be to learn how to think powerfully and accurately; that is the beginning of wisdom.

Creative thinking requires a disciplined mind.

LEVEL III: UNITY OF FUNCTION

The third type of order, "order for the sake of unity of function", is a higher level. Here, parts are organized and connected in such a way that they blend into a unified whole. The whole functions because of the harmonious blending of its parts.

An example of this type of order is a complex machine – the parts of the machine are connected in such a way that the machine functions properly. Each part would be useless on its own, but together they achieve their purpose.

The obvious question here is: what is the difference between this type of order and that of the previous level? Books in a library are correctly ordered according to the index, and parts of a machine are ordered according to the design of the machine – what is the significant difference?

But there is a world of difference: it is true that an index enables the function of the library as a whole, but each book in the library has its own separate identity and use – even if the index disappears and the books become completely disorganized, each book remains a book; you may have trouble locating it, but in itself it remains a book. However, in the case of a machine, the individual parts are *nothing* on their own; it is only in their combination that they achieve any meaning at all. In the library, the index makes each self-contained part accessible and therefore useful; but in the machine, the order and organization are the *entire reason* for the existence of the parts; no individual part has any use without all the others.

In an engine, for example, there may be a small screw which is almost insignificant in terms of its intrinsic value – it may be worth less than the smallest coin. But without it the engine does not run; and if that small screw falls out when the vehicle powered by that engine is in an inhospitable and dangerous place, the unfortunate driver will realize that that tiny screw is worth the value of the entire vehicle. Without that part he has nothing at all. While the engine was running smoothly that part was unconsidered and unappreciated; now that it is missing its value has become apparent.

Systems which are set up in such a way that all the parts are needed before any can function have a unique quality: each part reflects a paradox. Each part is both nothing and everything: nothing because it is only a part, without the rest of the system it is utterly useless; and everything because when all the other parts are in place and functioning, it becomes essential and critical. Each part depends on all the others entirely, in this it is utterly subservient; and yet all the others depend on it, in this it is utterly controlling.

MARRIAGE

The most potent and important learning experience for this depth is marriage. Marriage should be a relationship between two people in which each gives entirely to the other. Each one gives himself, herself entirely; utterly and fearlessly. The result is that something is built which far surpasses what each individual is as an individual, a combination of two souls each fuelled and fired by the other, far greater than each alone could have dreamed possible. And you can achieve this only if you are ready to give entirely with no thought of holding anything back, no reserve of any individual identity. You must be prepared to lose yourself completely in the relationship with total vulnerability. And the remarkable result is that when you give yourself away entirely, you discover yourself most sharply.

The paradox of this deepest of relationships is that to the degree you are willing to give yourself away, exactly to that degree you find yourself. And when you have found yourself thus clearly and sharply, you must be ready to put all that you have found, all that you have become, back into the relationship. You must give again, and more deeply. And again you will discover a new depth in your own inner being. And again you will give it away. That is the beginning of a relationship which can be called love.

That is the Jewish idea of marriage: two people giving so intensely that they find themselves each entirely within the essence of the other and yet each discovering a unique identity more sharply defined and more independent.

And it is easy to see that this is not the modern idea of marriage. A selfish generation does not know how to give, and real marriage, the real love that bonds two people into one fiery and shimmering bond of giving and discovery, is very hard to find.

In fact, the very idea of marriage as a commitment is not popular today. Who needs commitment? Why not enjoy the benefits of a relationship without its obligations? Relationships today are built on the shifting sands of self gratification: what is in this relationship for me? A relationship built on your self-interest is not a real relationship: it is simply a way of using someone for your needs; the deepest and most basic requirement for a real relationship is commitment! That is exactly what Jewish marriage is: an unconditional commitment. Only if you are prepared to give yourself entirely, body and soul, present and future, can you begin to talk about love.

THE JEWISH PEOPLE

The Jewish people constitute a system built on the third type of order. Each individual is essential and unique; *you* are absolutely necessary for the cosmic purpose which the Jewish nation must manifest. You are essential; the future of the entire Jewish nation depends on you. In that sense you are great beyond description. But when you are not fulfilling your destiny as part of that great and historic reality which is the Jewish people, you are lost and insignificant.

(In fact, on a broader scale, all of mankind and the Universe constitute such a system: everything in the world is created unique in its position and function and will ultimately reveal how critically necessary it is in the greater scheme of reality.)

When the Jewish people traveled through the desert they moved in formation – the "Flags of the Desert"; each tribe occupied a specific position within the camp. The root of this formation lies in the fact that each tribe has a specific identity and function within the Jewish people and therefore a specific place. Within each tribe, each family has a specific and unique role, and so too each individual within each family. As the Jewish people were being formed the uniqueness of each element within the nation was being laid down.

EMOTIONS AND INDIVIDUALITY

Because we are individuals who form a whole in such a way that each of us is critically important, we reflect this principle in our emotions. The human mind is a reflection of the deeper energies of Creation, and study of the mind yields a deep knowledge of the world.

It is a feature of our emotional nature that we respond both to the experience of being unique and single, and also to the experience of blending into a team or crew. Actually, these responses are contradictory: if it is natural to thrill to the experience of being a single, all-important individual, there should be a negative response to losing one's identity in a group; yet we find, paradoxically, that both are thrilling.

For example, in a situation where disaster is imminent, when everyone else is immobilized by fear or surprise and you act decisively, heroically and save the day unaided, such an event yields a great thrill; in fact, every young person has fantasized about such things. There is a special thrill in the awareness that the entire deliverance depended on you alone; the very aloneness of the individual in acting is the source of that unique surge of ego-experience.

A young man on the sports field, for example, will achieve heroic status if he manages to defeat the entire opposition team on his own at a critical moment in the match and score; this is the "lone ranger" syndrome in action. There is a great thrill in being the "loner", entirely independent and in no need of any outside assistance. This is the thrill of being a world unto yourself.

However, it is also a clear feature of human consciousness that we thrill to experiences in which the individual parts blend harmoniously in such a way that the parts become locked into the whole and lose their separate identity. A mass display of precision gymnastics in which no individual stands out but the entire human mass seems to function as one being, for example, evokes a special feeling in both the participants and the onlookers. Certain team sports which depend on perfect interaction between members of the team provide a unique thrill. In such activities, if one member were to make a small move expressing his particular individual existence, breaking the tight discipline of the team, the entire experience would be destroyed.

So we thrill to being single, alone and unique; and yet we also thrill to becoming part of a larger whole. We respond in these two opposite ways because that is exactly the nature and purpose of the human experience: each of us is unique, cosmically important; yet we achieve our uniqueness precisely when we fit into a larger order perfectly. Remarkably, it is exactly when we blend into the Universal picture exactly as we should in terms of our private, unique qualities and abilities that we thrill to the realization that no-one else could fulfill this particular function, no-one else could stand exactly here and do what must be done here. I fit in perfectly so that I become indistinguishable as an individual, and yet in so doing my individuality swells to the proportions of the Universe. *I am nothing, and yet I am everything.*

STEPS TO SELF-EXPRESSION

This knowledge can illuminate your path and help you define exactly what your role should be, exactly what your goal should be, in this world.

In order to begin the path of genuine self-development, you must learn to reject the mode of today's culture which sees the world as existing to serve the individual's self-interest.

You must look beyond yourself and you must look above yourself. If you cannot become a part of that which is around you and that which is above you, you can never become greater than your own personal limits. If you cannot really give of yourself to anyone or anything else, you will forever be alone in your undeveloped smallness. When you have begun to resolve the conflict of living as part of a greater reality and yet in that greater, expanded reality discover your own individual uniqueness, you have begun to walk the long road that leads to real maturity and real greatness.

So there are two phases: first, you must strive to discover your uniqueness. What is *your* particular task? What essential part of the world is yours to build? This question is critically important – a life spent pursuing some unrealistic and inappropriate goal is a life wasted, and worse, *it damages the entire world.* When that small and seemingly insignificant screw in that engine which we considered previously falls out of place and rattles around in the wrong part of the engine, the entire engine may be irreparably damaged.

(Defining your particular role in the world, discovering who you really are, is the subject of the next chapter.)

Second, you have to develop the depth to see that the thrill of fitting in is a much more mature experience than the thrill of being a loner at any cost. The immature personality *will choose to step out of line* in order to experience its own uniqueness; the fact that the overall structure is being betrayed and damaged is not relevant to such an undeveloped mind. Immaturity cannot see the beauty in yielding the self in order to actualize the self; in truth, however, that is the only way to genuine selfhood.

Chapter 5

Who Are You?
Defining Your Role in Life

How do you discover who you really are? What is your role in the world? What part must you play in the historic drama that is the story of the Jewish People? How do you fulfill yourself and live the most meaningful and perfect life possible?

DRAW A CIRCLE

Take a large sheet of clean, white paper. Draw a circle. In the circle, write down the features of your personality. Put in every aspect of your character, every talent you have. Be sure to include everything. You need to put in much more than the things that are recognized in the formal school system – all your personality traits must be clearly identified and included. Are you warm and empathic – do you find that others always seem to pour out their stories to you? Are you not that good with people but you have technical gifts – you understand tools and machines? Are you mainly intellectual or emotional? What are your tastes? What sort of person do you get on with? Are you talented? Musical? Athletic? Put in everything.

And then, outside the circle, write the things that you are not. There may be personal qualities or talents you wish you had, but if you lack them, write them down on the outside.

Study your circle and its contents. Study it well: you are looking at a picture of yourself. The real you; not the person you may fantasize about being but the real you. Outside the circle are your fantasies; inside is you.

If you want to know what you are meant to be doing in this world, look at your circle. The contents of that circle are your tools; your task is to use those tools to their maximum. If those are the tools you have been given, they define your role and your life's work.

If you were placed on a building site with a bag of tools by an intelligent foreman, all you need do is look around and see what is being built in your immediate vicinity and what tools you have been given and you will know immediately what you should be doing. Obviously, you have been given exactly the tools you need for the job; life is not a joke – you have a task to accomplish and you have most definitely been given all that you need to accomplish it. *A careful examination of your place in the world and your personal character tools will give you a clear picture of who you are and what you must do.*

If you think you lack the tools you need for life, you are wrong. You are mistaken either because you have those tools but you are simply unaware of them, or you are mistaken about your task in life: you have the tools you need to fulfill your role but you are pursuing the wrong role. The role you imagine to be yours is in fact someone else's. In other words, you are unaware of your tools, or you are unaware of your role. You need to do some serious work to discover exactly the nature of your tools (and to discover all of them; nothing has been given to you to be wasted). And you need to do some serious work to discover your role; *stop longing for someone else's role* and get busy finding yours.

Again, the tools match the job exactly. We understand that the One who creates the whole enterprise gives every individual exactly what he or she needs to carry out the work that is necessary.

So study your circle well. You will experience joy: if you have correctly identified your real character, you will experience the joy of recognizing yourself clearly, identifying yourself where you may have been confused before. If you have ever really wondered about who you are and what you should be doing in life, you will feel a great happiness in seeing the answer to those questions before you.

And if you have ever felt jealous of anyone who has gifts or talents that you wish you had, *you will lose that jealousy:* if they have been given those talents it is only because they need them for their role. If you do not have those particular gifts, it is because you do not need them – you have been given the tools you need; you could not use someone else's tools because they are irrelevant to your life's purpose. That person needs them; you do not.

EXPLORING THE CIRCLE

Let us look more closely at the process of drawing the circle that is the picture of your personality and defines your direction in life.

There are two phases in life:

The first is the phase of your childhood and teenage years, during which your work is *to discover what your talents and abilities are;* to put into the circle every element that belongs there.

The first phase ends when you *close the circle;* to do this you must see clearly what belongs inside the circle and what belongs outside and to develop the maturity to see that what belongs outside *must be left out* no matter how much you would like to have those elements inside.

The second phase is the rest of your life: after you have closed the circle and defined exactly who you are, your work consists of spending the rest of your life *becoming the world's greatest master* of that combination of abilities that is your circle. Every moment of the rest of your life should be spent developing and perfecting every aspect of your unique personality and bringing it to total expression.

Let us look at each of these stages.

PHASE ONE: OPEN THE CIRCLE

Youth is given in order to discover your abilities. By the time you are eighteen or thereabouts, you should be aware of your talents and general abilities. You should have a good feel for those areas in which you are strong; these are usually things that you like and do well. How do you ensure that you have in fact discovered all that you must? What elements are essential in the process of self-discovery?

Self-awareness: You need to develop confidence in your own knowledge of yourself. You need to learn to look objectively at yourself and decide what the most important features of your personality are. No amount of advice or counsel from others can substitute for your own healthy self-awareness, and ultimately, it is this faculty which must be developed. You must build deep and objective insight.

Torah learning: Torah learning is a key to self-knowledge. Torah is the definition of objectivity; the Torah reflects the world accurately and therefore learning Torah and incorporating it into your mind is a fundamental method of developing powerful clarity and objectivity.

Also, since the main cause of our lack of objectivity is our lower self, our character weakness, Torah is necessary in order to gain insight because the end result of Torah learning is character growth. In other words, the undeveloped and immature mind cannot be objective, and Torah learning is the prime method of developing mental maturity and depth. This requires Torah study aimed at personal growth; simply learning Torah at the intellectual level is not enough. You need a program of deep learning which includes study and work specifically in those aspects of Torah which train the character.

However, even this is not enough. No-one can be entirely objective about the self, and therefore you need a guide. The Torah is clear on this: you need a Rebbe; someone who is greater than you, more objective about life and the world, and more experienced. And someone who is ready and able to tell you the truth about yourself.

Sometimes, a sensitive and talented schoolteacher can help. Often, parents can help; parents may not be completely objective about their children, but they are usually far more objective about many aspects of your character than you are.

So you must explore. You cannot afford to miss a talent; you need to discover every gift and every aspect of your natural abilities. Of course, we are seeking to explore and discover in ways that are safe – every ability must be explored and developed without leaving any scars. Relationships, in particular, must be carefully conducted; you do not want to explore an area in such a way that it is left damaged or desensitized. Torah guidance is absolutely essential here.

GIFTS FOR EXPLORATION AND DISCOVERY

You will note that youth has the special characteristic of loving exploration and discovery. Young people have the confident belief that all roads are open, there are no limitations. Young children believe that they will be the world's greatest in any field they care to enter. They have no sense of the limitations imposed by practical matters; that comes later in life. This sense of wonder and openness is a gift; children and young teenagers are given this as a tool to enable them to open all the areas of their potential. And it does not last; many adults feel quite the opposite: that life has closed in on them and imposed strict limits; limitations of time, money, energy or other forms of limitation. Youth is the time when you need this feeling of the unlimited; that is when you must use it.

So use your sense of freedom well. Use it to discover all that lies within yourself, all your hidden potential.

THE CIRCLE STANDS ON A BASE

Of course, there are some basics we all need. Before you begin the serious work of defining your unique circle, there are some fundamental qualities you need to acquire. Your circle stands on a base which is essential, and that base has two parts:

First, you must be a decent, refined human being. And second, you must live up to your Jewish obligations. These are the universal qualities and elements that are necessary before your circle can become meaningful: we all need to be working on self-control and refining our characters. We all need to learn consideration and concern and many other qualities. The circle is the unique constellation of features that makes each of us distinct, but before you work on becoming distinct you need to be sure that the basics are in place so that your circle has a place to stand.

As an illustration: certain basic requirements of clothing must be met before you can consider the question of personal style – you must ensure that you have the essential items of clothing needed to be decently covered before you turn your attention to the particular style of those clothes that appeals to you: you would look ridiculous choosing elements of style in your clothing if you are not yet decently covered! First, the basics must be in place; then one can begin expressing personal taste and style.

But once you have included the basic human and Jewish elements into your personal program of growth, then you must focus on the elements of your own personal style.

CLOSING THE CIRCLE

Now comes the hard part: at some point, the circle must be closed. You cannot begin to achieve while you are still exploring and deciding where to invest your life's energy. And the problem is that we do not like to close circles; we like to keep all possibilities open. It is very difficult to admit that you are not going to achieve something that has the appeal of childhood fantasy. It is very difficult to admit that a number of possibilities must be sacrificed forever. Let us study this.

Because the natural mode of childhood is to believe that everything is possible, because the child is certain that he can and will be anything and everything he wants to be, the immature side of our nature remains attached to that world of potential. *Maturity means realizing that in order to have what you can have, you have to sacrifice all the alternatives.*

For a man to get married, he must sacrifice a relationship with every woman on earth except the one he marries. The immature mind focuses on the fantasy of all those other relationships; the mature mind focuses on the beauty of the relationship which will be built with the woman he marries.

The immature mind would rather have nothing as long as it can live in the fantasy that all is possible; the mature mind is ready to give up the illusion of open potential to achieve and have that limited amount that it is possible to have. The immature mind dwells on the excitement of dreaming of every relationship that could be *and has none;* the mature mind closes the circle, chooses the best that can be chosen and *has that which is real.*

Again, immaturity means dreaming of all the options and actualizing none; maturity means achieving the wisdom to understand that all the options must be sacrificed except those that can become real. In fact, the false options must be sacrificed *so that* the genuine ones can become real.

A child cannot understand this. A child lives in the belief that all is his. A child cannot sacrifice the total range of possibilities to have what he can have. Have you ever seen a child standing outside a delicatessen clutching a coin in his hand, dreamily examining all the delicious-looking buns in the window? That is a happy child; he may stand there for ages enjoying the process of choosing which he is going to buy. But when he has finally decided and is about to hand over his money and receive the bun he has chosen, a strange thing happens. Suddenly, all the other buns look more delicious than the one he has chosen. Before, they all glittered with promise; now, the one he has chosen becomes dull and all the others begin to glow brightly! That is a miserable child; he cannot handle the knowledge that he cannot have all.

If a child is holding two ice creams so that his hands are full, and then he is offered a third, you will see the agony on his face. In fact, the result will probably be a heap of ice cream and tears on the ground as the child tries somehow to hold all three – he cannot give up any potential option.

This is a deep problem; we are all that child. We tend to focus on the promise of infinite potential rather than the reality of finite achievement. But the nature of the world is that in order to achieve anything, all potential must be sacrificed. You must pay away the money to buy the goods, you cannot have both the money and what it can buy. This is a finite world of limited options; the problem is to decide which are the correct ones to pursue.

Picture the visitor to a vacation resort with one day to enjoy. He wakes early intent on getting the most out of the day: there are rivers to swim, lakes to sail, mountains to climb. But one day is enough to do only one of those things, not all of them. The mature individual makes a decision; for better or worse, without knowing which activity will really turn out to be the best, he must choose one. And so he does, and gets on with it and does it fully. But the immature individual, the childish person, may spend most of the day trying to decide! Each activity seems more attractive than the next, and a good decision seems impossible. And very often this type of person *will not enjoy whatever option he chooses;* whatever he does he will be sure that the others would have been better!

And that is life. You cannot do it all. The world beckons with so many options, so much beauty and so much power. *But only the part of it that is really your unique part is real;* you must never forget that. You must rapidly decide what is for you, and then get on with it and not look back. You must claim your part of the world's work and do it as if that is all there is. The rest belongs to others; take care of your part and the rest will be done. Sooner or later, but it will all be done; and when it is, your part will glow in the entirety of the structure, and your experience will swell to the proportions of the universe.

Potential must be translated into the actual. The potential is exciting, appealing, infinite. The actual is so limited by comparison. That is our problem.

This tension between potential and actual exists in all aspects of life:

Money: money is power, rich potential. In fact, that is all money is. And therein lies its attraction – if I have a lot of money, I have a lot of potential, a lot of options. And that is why many people want money even if they do not intend to buy any specific thing: it is the power of unlimited options that appeals. But a mature individual is interested in money only for what it buys; such a person will be happy with enough money for his real needs and when he has the required amount for any particular need, he spends it and buys the needed item. He is happy to give away the potential for the goods.

Life itself: the happiness of the birth of a child is that a life of potential has begun, a whole life lies ahead. True, this newborn child has not achieved anything yet, but the moment is happy – he has a lifetime in which to achieve, the options seem almost unlimited. And old age: that is sad because the options have shrunk, the old person has very little power, very few options left, perhaps only enough strength to turn his chair a little closer to the sun. And the end of life itself is the ultimate closing of all potential entirely.

But that is not the Jewish view. We regard birth as happy, yes; the potential is enormous and of course it is essential. But this child has achieved nothing yet, he has acquired nothing of the world and built none of his character and spirit.

In fact, this is an anxious moment. And old age in the Jewish view: certainly, potential has shrunk, but this person has achieved!

If this old person who sits almost powerless at the end of a lifetime has spent every day of life achieving, building, working to develop the inner self of the mind and spirit as well as the outer world, this old age is not sad; on the contrary: the money has been spent but *the goods have been bought!* Those goods of character, of Torah and correct actions which have been built during a lifetime of toil have been acquired, they are forever. What a different view of life! Our view of life is that it gets happier as it progresses, happier as potential is converted to reality, not sadder as options close and old age approaches.

In the literature of the world, youth is always described as springtime and summer, and old age as winter. After all, spring is when things are moving, happening, in nature and winter is when things are slowing down. But in Torah, it is just the opposite: youth is described as winter and old age as summer! King Solomon talks of "The days of my winter" when referring to his youth. And the reason should be obvious: in the winter the hard ground is broken and the seeds are planted, but nothing has grown yet; in the summer the crop is ready for reaping! That is the correct view of life; and the only one that can prevent the sadness and gloom of life's gradual ebbing deepening as it progresses.

So we must learn to close the circle. As long as we insist on keeping that circle open, keeping all possibilities alive always, we can achieve nothing.

They tell a story about a peasant farmer in old Russia. This poor individual stood weeping by the roadside, a farmer with no land to farm. As he stood there without a future, the Czar happened to ride past in his royal coach. He saw the peasant and his tears and was moved to stop and ask the cause of the man's grief. When he heard that the problem was the lack of land to farm, he drove a stake into the ground where they stood and gave the overawed peasant three similar stakes, telling him to walk as far as he wished and then to drive a second stake into the earth, turn, walk on again as far as he wished, plant a third, turn and walk again until he had gone as far as he wanted, and then to plant the fourth stake. The land between the four stakes would be his, a personal gift from the Czar.

The man was overcome with joy and began walking. After he had gone some distance he stopped and prepared to drive a stake into the ground, when he said to himself: "Why should I stop here? I could have more," and continued walking. After a while he stopped again and was about to plant a stake and turn, when again he said: "Why stop here?"

And as the story goes, he never stopped walking.

PHASE TWO: BUILDING

When the circle is closed, when you know who you are and what you must do, that is the time to get moving. Now you must move ahead to develop all that is in your circle to its maximum depth and beauty. That is the work of the rest of your life – to achieve unlimited greatness in that combination of qualities that is your unique identity.

The trick is to retain the memory of the excitement of youth, the wonder of the moments of discovering your uniqueness, and to carry that freshness with you always. Your circle must remain clear in your mind and the joy of discovering it must accompany you through a lifetime of focused building.

Chapter 6

Freedom and Responsibility

M odern society values freedom. The charters and constitutions of democracies enshrine freedom in every possible form. The idea of obligation is not popular at all in this age.

It is fundamental to understand that a refined and developed person is one *who has a sense of obligation.* One who feels the responsibility of living up to the highest standards, one who feels obliged to honor his or her commitments, one who feels obliged by the truth, that is a person worth knowing and trusting.

You cannot trust someone who has no sense of obligation. When you are considering marriage, one of the most important qualities to seek in your prospective partner is a deep sense of responsibility. A carefree spirit who does not feel obliged by anything may be attractive, but do not marry such a person.

In business and friendships too, this quality is essential. The foundation of a solid personality is the sense of commitment, the idea of fulfilling obligations, the ability to take responsibility. If you develop strength in this area in a world which is very weak in this and you seek relationships with others who understand and work on this aspect of their characters, you will avoid many problems and give yourself a chance to build a life worth living.

JEWISH OBLIGATION, JEWISH FREEDOM

The idea of freedom has taken on almost absolute value in society. Even in the Jewish world there are attempts to apply this ideology – movements which attempt to change Judaism cut one obligation after another until there is no obligation left at all.

But Judaism without obligation is a contradiction in terms. In fact, the very idea of a spiritual path requires obligation: if there is a higher world of truth, it must oblige. What could be the meaning of a truth that stands above this physical world but does not oblige us to live according to its standard? If there is a definition of right and wrong above and beyond my human mind, then I am obliged by it. If I create my own definition of right and wrong, obviously it can never be greater than my understanding, and obviously it cannot oblige me – if I am free to create my own rules then I am free to change them and break them too.

If *I* decide what my obligations are, of course those obligations are really only a thin veil for my own ego. The concept of obligation means that I am obliged *whether I wish it or not;* you cannot say that you are obliged if you constantly choose your own "obligations". As long as you can reject those "obligations" they are not binding at all.

Torah is pure obligation. Torah commands, obliges. *And yet it is exactly here, in the realm of deep obligation, that freedom is to be found.* Real freedom means living in harmony with the truth. A fierce loyalty to the truth – that is real freedom. Any other sense of freedom is an illusion.

Only a slave to the truth is free.

GIVING AND TAKING

Let us look more deeply into the opposing views of Torah and modern society regarding the idea of obligation. In order to do this, we shall need to understand a classic Torah idea, the idea of giving and taking.

All relationships between people involve giving and taking. In some aspects of a relationship one person is the giver and the other receives, and in some aspects the direction of giving is the reverse. Any particular individual relates to others, and in fact to the world in general, by means of giving and taking, and here we have one of the most important insights into character – some people are givers, some are takers.

In their depth, these two polarities represent the higher, spiritual world and the lower, material world. Giving is an attribute of the Divine; in fact, it is the primary quality of

Hashem to which we can relate. Taking is foreign to the Divine; taking implies some lack, some need which is fulfilled by that which is given – obviously this is not relevant to the Creator who lacks nothing. One who gives resembles the Divine; one who takes distances himself from his Divine image.

"One who hates gifts shall live." One who loves to give is living in parallel with the higher attributes; one who loves to receive is in conflict with that ideal. Giving is an aspect of goodness and self-sufficiency; taking is a symptom of lack and deficiency. One who loves taking, who is in the habit of taking, is training himself to live in a vacuum of lack and dependency.

Of course, sometimes receiving is actually giving – a great person's acceptance of a gift from an admirer is in fact an act of giving; in such a case it is the giver who *needs* to give, the receiver does not need the gift but accepts it only as a favor to the giver. In such a case, the receiver of the gift is the real giver. What is important is the essence of the transaction and the relationship, not the transfer of a physical object. In an ideal relationship, for example an ideal marriage, both parties know how to give and also how to receive graciously; one of the deepest gifts in marriage is the opportunity you give your partner to be a giver!

RIGHTS AND OBLIGATIONS

Giving and taking. Now the application of this fundamental subject which sheds light on modern society (and the Jew's place in it) is as follows. In human relationships, giving and taking can be expressed as *obligations* and *rights*. My rights are your obligations: my right to my property can be expressed as your obligation not to steal. My right to free speech is your obligation to allow me to speak freely. A worker's right to a living wage is his employer's obligation to pay that wage. It is your obligation to see to it that my rights remain intact. Every right implies an obligation; the rights of individuals are the obligations of society at large.

The important point to grasp here is that rights and obligations are interlocked; neither is meaningful without the other. Just as there can be no receiver without a giver, there can be no rights without obligations.

In fact, rights are parallel to taking, and obligations are parallel to giving. After all, my rights are due *to me*, I can demand them if necessary, they are *mine*. Obligations are those things which I have to do *for you*, I have to limit myself, to *give up* some of my freedom and desires in order to accommodate your rights. *In guarding my rights I am a taker; in honoring my obligations I am a giver.*

Of course, both rights and obligations are true and necessary. You do have a right to expect that which is due to you and an obligation to provide others with all that is due to them. But the essential question is: *where is your focus?* What concerns you more – your rights or your obligations? *A person who is concerned with his rights is a taker; one who is concerned with his obligations is a giver.* Focusing on your rights is focusing on yourself – a constant awareness of your needs and the desire to satisfy them. Focusing on your obligations is focusing on others and the function of giving.

This difference of focus has far-reaching practical consequences. Picture the ideal relationship between employer and worker: the worker must work for his employer as best he is able, and the employer must treat his worker as a brother. Obviously, if both live up to their obligations the relationship will be productive and peaceful. But when the employer focuses on the worker's obligation to work hard, and the worker keeps demanding that the employer treat him better – when each one forgets his obligations and thinks only of his rights – the result is war. When the employer reminds the worker that he is supposed to work single-mindedly and the worker reminds the employer that he is supposed to treat him like a brother, both are absolutely correct – *but they are focusing on the wrong end of the deal,* and *that* is where the problems begin.

In an industrial society, when employers treat employees fairly and the workers serve loyally, all is well. But when workers are concerned primarily about their rights, the natural result is that in order to protect and enforce their rights they band together in a union. The union has the power to paralyze an industry, so the employers form a national association of employers to fight the stranglehold of the union, and the result is battle.

MAN, WOMAN AND COMMITMENT

Imagine two people in marriage, each trying to give to the other – the result is a perfect relationship. But two people, each focusing on what *the other* owes – the result is marital strife. The surest way to lose your personal happiness is to demand it as a right from your spouse.

Marriage is the main learning experience in the area of giving and taking. It is here, perhaps more than anywhere else, that being a giver is all-important. Modern society develops people who are conscious of their rights, and modern marriage is in trouble. The Jewish idea of marriage is that it should be approached as an experience of pure giving. Of course, as we have already pointed out, you should choose a partner who understands this secret too; if you do so, and then take care that your entire focus in the relationship is giving, you will succeed. Not only succeed; you will achieve greatness. And your home will be a shining example of Jewish values.

RIGHTS AND OBLIGATIONS IN SOCIETY

Modern society is largely concerned with rights. The wording of the constitutions of Western democracies is very revealing – they focus on rights; in fact, they are often little more than a detailed list of the rights of the individuals in that particular society. The highest code of such societies is their Bill of Rights.

In striking contrast is the Torah, the Jewish Constitution. *The Torah never mentions rights,* only obligations! Nowhere does the Torah speak of your right to your property; only your obligation not to steal. No mention of a right to life or liberty; only stringent admonitions not to kill or interfere with the liberty of others. Not even a cursory mention of a right to happiness, dignity, physical well-being or sustenance; only strong reminders of the duty to provide others with these. And so on.

Of course rights exist; of course they are important. The Oral Law is full of discussions of individual rights. But the point is that the focus is everything. In a perfect society, which is the inevitable result of meticulous Torah observance, individuals consider and live up to their obligations. When each person watches his obligations carefully, *the rights take care of themselves.* If no-one steals, everyone's right to property is assured automatically. If no-one interferes with anyone, everyone's freedom is the result. When people are givers, happiness results.

When everyone is giving, everyone receives.

A society which focuses on rights is a society which develops takers. A society which focuses on obligations develops givers. The specific details of a political system are far less important than this basic idea; in fact, *no* political system will work when the individuals in that system are inherently takers – they will always be trying to take what they can from the system, and they will always feel that they are not getting enough. Conversely, almost any political system will work admirably when its members are careful to contribute at least as much as they receive.

The great secret of political and social stability is that the *individuals* within a system must be givers. The Torah insists on this; a child raised in a Torah environment is a child who is trained to be conscious of his obligations. Such a member of society can be relied upon, even when no-one is watching!

Many people think that the reason we must maintain our obligations is so that society can function: after all, if I behave violently and immorally, others will do so too, and chaos will result. In other words, in order to maintain peace and order, morality is necessary. This is known as reciprocity: I must behave correctly so that you will, too, and the result will be that we both benefit.

But a little thought will show you that this is not good enough. Firstly, you can see that the real interest here is selfish: for my own benefit I am prepared to control myself;

my behaving correctly and treating you fairly is for the purpose of making sure that you treat me fairly. What I am really interested in is my own good. Someone who thinks this way is not a genuine giver; in fact, that person is really a taker.

But worse than that, this idea will not work: the idea of behaving correctly so that others will do so too makes sense only in those situations where there is a danger of influencing others – for example, where I am being watched. When others observe me, I shall behave correctly because I must maintain the fabric of a decent society; I must be sure to play the game by the rules so that others will play by the rules, too. But what will happen when no-one is watching? What will happen when I am tempted to be dishonest in a private and secret situation where no-one will ever know that a wrong was committed? Surely one who plays by the rules only so that others must will not control himself when a secret immorality beckons? After all, if no-one will ever know, and if no-one will ever break the rules as a result, why should I not do so?

No; only a strong personal morality is adequate to ensure that society functions morally. Only when the individuals in a community or society feel personally obliged to do that which is right can there be genuine morality.

Whether we are talking about a relationship between two people or a relationship among millions in a society, only the personal sense of obligation of each individual will be enough to ensure real good. Relationships and cultures depend on the genuine, personal and private quality of their individuals.

There is no alternative: either you work on yourself in the most genuine and deep way, or your world will be chaos. Either you must perfect your own inner world or the outer world will break down.

SELF-DEFENSE

Of course, there is a very important condition which must apply before any individual can give fully and unconditionally in society: everyone else must do so too! If you try to live up to your obligations with no regard to your rights in a society of takers, you will be swallowed alive. It is therefore the aim of Torah education to produce an individual who is a giver, but who knows how to protect himself from the unscrupulous when that is necessary.

Being a full-hearted giver does not mean being naive about the realities of society; Torah openly discusses the crookedness of the evil and teaches appropriate self-defense. When Jacob lives with Laban who is a swindler and a cheat, Jacob has to subdue his inner core of pure giving and deal with Laban on his own terms in order to survive and succeed; his greatness, however, is that it leaves him inwardly untainted. In the privacy of the Jewish heart and family, pure giving is the appropriate mode; in a murderous and perverse environment, self-defense is necessary – *but it must never affect the core.*

Many people are mistaken about this: they believe that a true Torah education will produce naive, unsophisticated individuals. Perhaps children should be exposed to the harsh realities of the outside world from the beginning so that they will be at ease within it? How will the products of a Torah education handle the "real world" when they leave the shelter of their religious homes and communities to interact with that world? How will they react to the realities of immorality and dishonesty in the outside world? Will they not be shocked or perhaps dangerously affected by it? Are they not totally unprepared for it?

But nothing could be more mistaken. Children who receive a genuine Jewish education *are exposed to the immorality and evils of the world:* the Torah contains every imaginable form of immorality, perversion and dishonesty, described and analyzed in great detail! From the very beginning, the youngest students of Torah learn about these things; *but they learn about them with their correct attitude and interpretation.* Such students are not shocked to discover that the world contains the worst immoralities and evils: they have met these from the beginning. In fact, they have probably had a more comprehensive education about the world's lower side than the child in a secular environment who may have no systematic, organized education about these things at all.

A real education in morality requires knowing the enemy: you must know the worst of human possibilities in order to fight the battle of morality. Of course a Torah education must do this; but it must first give the sense of goodness and morality that is necessary to approach this dangerous area correctly armed and prepared. And the only really effective weapons are the inner ones: a deep knowledge of right and wrong and an unshakable commitment to that which is right.

NOW AND LATER

Let us look more deeply into the idea of giving and taking. Of course, when you give, you benefit tremendously. Of course you receive as a result of your giving. It is virtually impossible to give with no personal benefit, no personal taking of some kind. In fact, giving is the very best thing you can do *for you,* for your own personal gain. Every act of giving has many benefits for the giver. So what is the difference between giving and taking? What is the real difference if I receive every time I give? In practice, why is giving greater than taking if giving is really the best I can do for myself?

This needs thought. You will find great reward in answering this question for yourself; but one avenue of insight (and there are others which are deeper) is this:

Taking is related to the present – when I take, I have what I want now. Giving is an investment in the future – when I give, apart from the pleasure of giving, I may not see the effects for a long time; in fact, all I may experience now is the sacrifice of that which I am giving away. A Jewish life is invested in the future; that is the meaning of *emuna,* faith. I do what I must because it is correct, because I am obliged; I am not looking for an immediate result. The focus on giving and obligation is a focus on another time and another world. Just as the farmer plants seeds and tends them while the crop is yet a season distant, so too the person of *emuna* plants in this world and knows that in another time and another season the fruits will result.

This is the path of maturity; but the immature mind is always seeking a "quick fix", immediate gratification. We have already observed that our generation is intent on "quick fixes". Things that demand time and patience are not popular. That which is not "instant" does not sell, and patience is a thing of the past.

The need for instant gratification is a symptom of immaturity, and it stems in depth from the focus on self and the taking which serves that self. The long-forgotten art of patience is an excellent training for maturity and true depth, and it is necessary for building a personality whose natural mode is giving.

OBLIGATION AND GREATNESS

There is another depth in the idea of obligation. "One who is commanded and does is greater than one who is not commanded and does." In other words, one who does because he is commanded is greater than one who acts spontaneously. But why? Surely spontaneity is greater? Surely an action that is generated within yourself is greater than an action performed because you are obliged from without?

One of the classic answers to this question is that when you are commanded to act, you are immediately confronted by resistance – your own lower self steps in and says "Don't tell me what to do!" The ego, the "I", that deep root of the personality wishes to assert itself, refuses to be subdued. Therefore, in order to fulfill a command you must overcome this inner resistance, and in doing so lies the secret of inner growth – self-control is at the heart of all personal growth. However, when you act spontaneously there is no resistance to overcome and the action is easy; it is not intrinsically an exercise in self-control and therefore has relatively little growth potential.

But there is more here. When you act spontaneously, motivated only by that which arises within yourself, you are expressing yourself. That may be great, but it can never be greater than you are at the moment you act. At best, the act will be a full and true expression of all that you are. But when the command originates outside of yourself and you fulfill it, something is happening which expresses more than just yourself. When you act because you are commanded by a source outside of yourself, you become the expression of that source. Your action is an expression of the command of the source, and *you are an expression of the source itself.* In fact, you and that source become one: both are needed for the result to manifest – the point of origin of the process and its completion in the final action.

When you fulfill a command that comes from a higher world you are expressing the level of that world, you rise to a level far beyond yourself. When you act in fulfilling a commandment you are no less than a partner with the Divine; you have locked into the infinite dimension and you reveal in the world what the Source of that action intends to reveal. The word *mitzva,* commandment, is based on a root meaning "together", partners. When you perform a *mitzva* you form a partnership with the One who commands it – He desires a certain result and commands it; you express it in the world. He is the beginning of the process, you are its completion. *Together* you accomplish it. Far greater is the one who acts because he is commanded!

The secret depth here is that in overcoming your private, limited self, *because* you overcome that individual self, you expand to a greater level, you reach into a higher world.

OBLIGATION AND STRUCTURE – THE POWER TO THINK CLEARLY

The vessel in the personality which holds the sense of obligation is an ordered mind. A disorganized, disintegrated personality does not sense being obliged.

Only a clear-thinking mind can grasp the essence of truth. The truth is ultimately limited – there are many false answers to any particular problem, infinitely many. But the truth is limited; it derives from the world of Oneness, its nature is to be one. *There are many falsehoods but only one truth.* In this, truth is the ultimate constraint, and in this, too, truth is the ultimate freedom. The disorganized mind wanders in falsehoods. There is no limit to the number of false paths that the undisciplined mind can wander. The organized, structured mind pursues paths that are true and *only* paths that are true. Such a mind perceives an obligation to the truth.

Only a slave to the truth is free.

Chapter 7

Getting High, Staying High

Why do the good times never last? Why are things so good when they are fresh but always become stale? Why is the beginning of a relationship so exciting but the later stages often so dull? Why do we feel things so sharply at first but become so easily bored?

There is a deep secret here and understanding it can change your life. Trying to go through life without knowing it guarantees disappointment, and understanding it well can change potential disaster into real happiness.

THE TWO PHASES OF ALL EXPERIENCE

The natural pathway of all life experiences begins with inspiration and soon fades to disappointment.

Our senses are tuned to an initial burst of sensitivity and then rapidly decay into dullness. Sights, sounds and smells are felt sharply at first and then hardly at all – a constant sound is not noticed; you suddenly become aware that it was present when it stops! We are incapable of maintaining the freshness of any experience naturally.

One of the Torah sources for this idea lies in the sequence of events surrounding the exodus from Egypt. At an extremely low point in our history, during the intense misery of slavery in Egypt, literally at the point of spiritual annihilation, we were uplifted miraculously. Ten plagues revealed Hashem's presence and power, ending in a night alive with revelation. This spiritual high was amplified at the splitting of the sea – there the lowliest of the Jewish people experienced more than the highest prophet ever did later. But suddenly, once through the sea, we were deposited in a desert with many days of work ahead of us to climb to the Sinai experience, the giving of the Torah.

A desert means a place of intense death-forces, a place of lethal ordeals. No water means no life. In other words, that journey of the Jewish people began with the high of the exodus and ended with the giving of the Torah at Sinai, but there was a desert between those two points. A high beginning and an even higher end, but a desert in between.

What is the meaning of this pattern? The idea is that in order to save the Jewish people in Egypt outside help was necessary. Hashem appeared and elevated us spiritually *although we did not deserve it, we had not yet earned it.* We were taken out through no effort of our own, the journey began with a "free ride"; but it ended in success only because of the work we did. First, there is a free ride; then the work begins.

And that is the story of life. Experiences that are easy at first become difficult later. Things begin with a sense of freshness and inspiration, but the work must be done, inspiration does not last.

Once you are inspired the price must be paid, the experience must be earned, and in working to earn the level which was given *artificially,* you *acquire* that level genuinely. After being *shown* a spiritual level, you must *reach* it.

That is the secret. We are inspired artificially at the beginning of any phase of life, but to acquire the depth of personality that is demanded of us, *the inspiration is removed.* The danger is apathy and depression; the challenge is to fight back to the point of inspiration, and in so doing to *build it permanently into your character.* The plagues in Egypt and the splitting of the sea are dazzling beyond description, but then we are dropped in the desert and challenged to fight through to Sinai. In Egypt Hashem demonstrates destruction of ten levels of evil while we watch passively; in the desert He brings ten levels of evil against us and challenges *us* to destroy them. The ten plagues in Egypt were easy – we did nothing but witness them. The ten fearful ordeals that we faced in the desert years were immensely difficult. First, the process is made easy, inspiration is guaranteed; then inspiration is removed, the only guarantee that remains is that things will be difficult.

But of course, *that is where you really grow;* while things are easy all you have is the illusion that they will always remain easy. When things get difficult and you have to cope and battle to survive, when the illusion crumbles, that is when you begin real growth.

Why is this the pathway? Why must there be these two phases? The answer is that you must be uplifted in order to know your capabilities; you must be shown what you could be in order to feel inspired enough to work for it through all the ordeals that must be experienced to get there. You could not enter the battle if there were no inspiration first; you would be without energy, without fire. So first there is the inspiration, the energizing beginning. And just when you are sure it will go on forever, the cruel letdown strikes.

LEARNING TO WALK

Perhaps the best analogy is a father teaching his child to walk: first the father supports the child and lifts him gently to his feet. As he holds the child's hands and the child takes his first ecstatic step he is filled with a sense of power and exhilaration; in his young, inexperienced mind he is walking! *And he cannot fall:* his father is holding him.

But then the father must let go; there is no other way to learn. The child must take a frightened and lonely step unaided. And at the moment when he finds himself unsupported he feels a cruel stab of pain and fear: the one he trusted has let go. He has been lured into this situation of danger, and now he must manage on his own. He is forced to take the next step alone. And it is then that he learns to walk.

But then, and only then, when he is walking independently, can he feel his father's love in the very moment which previously felt like desertion. Only then does he realize that in the moment that felt like desertion was a greater love than in the moment of support. The moment of his father's letting go and allowing him to stand on his own was a far more profound moment of love than any other. And only then can he rush into his father's arms in real understanding.

First, it was necessary to hold and lift him, he would not have learned otherwise; first, he had to be shown. But then, when the lesson has been taught, he has to be left on his own, and that is where he learned to walk.

First, it is done for you. Then, you must do it yourself. The child in you must be nurtured and suckled; but when it is time to become an adult you must fight for yourself.

Unfortunately most people do not know this secret. We think that the world is supposed to be a constant thrill and we feel only half-alive because it is not. We crave the moments of uplift, the free rides, and we dread the moments of seeming abandonment and letdown. And if you do not understand that *you are never abandoned* your life can be a living hell of fear and pain.

But if you realize that in every moment of difficulty, every moment of independent struggle you are learning to walk, your hands are just out of contact with His and He is waiting for that embrace as you walk and then run independently, life can be a process of maintained inspiration despite its ordeals, and in fact, *because of its ordeals.*

Let us examine some applications of this fundamental principle.

THE UNBORN CHILD

The child is taught the whole Torah in the womb. An angel teaches him all the mysteries of Creation and all that he will ever need to know to reach perfection. A lamp is lit above his head and by its light he sees from one end of the world to the other. As the child is born, however, the angel strikes him on the mouth and he forgets all that he has learned and is born a simple and unlearned baby. The obvious question is: why teach a child so much and then cause all the teaching to be forgotten?

But the answer is that it is not forgotten; it is driven deep into the unconscious. You are born with no explicit knowledge, but beneath the conscious surface, intact and rich beyond imagination, is *all that you will ever need to know.* That is why when you hear something beautiful and true you have the sensation, not of learning something, but of *recognizing* something! And if you are sensitive you will feel your deep intuitive level often.

A lifetime of hard work learning Torah and working on your personality will constantly release, bring to the surface, your inborn wisdom.

The pathway is clear – you are born with a lifetime of work ahead; spiritual wisdom and growth are hard to earn. *But the inspiration is within;* you were once there! And that inner sense of inspiration provides the motivation, the source of optimism and confidence that genuine achievement is possible, even assured, if you make the effort.

CHILD AND TEENAGER

A second application: a feature of childhood and the teenage years is inspired optimism and the lack of a sense of limitation. Children believe that they can become anything. The world is larger-than-life to a child, a child is not oppressed by a limited sense of what is possible. A child has simply to be exposed to almost any form of greatness to begin fantasizing about becoming or achieving that same thing.

However, later in life one is lucky to have any inspiration left at all. Many adults wonder why life seemed so rich when they were teenagers, why they could laugh or cry so richly, so fully, back then; and why life seems so flat now. But the idea is as we have described above. First comes a phase of *unreal* positivity, a charge of energy. And then life challenges one to climb back to real achievement independently.

So be warned. The energy you feel now may not last. The idealism and power you feel now may wind down; that is what usually happens. *Unless you make an effort;* unless you prepare. The energy that drives you now is a gift; it is given so that you will feel motivated to achieve, to build yourself into all that you can be. Use it well; use it to leap into the rest of your life with confidence and freshness so that it will not fade, not even when the going gets rough. Learn to use your resources so well that you become self-motivated and self-generating. Remember the inspiration; savor it and enjoy it while you have it and *learn how to take it with you.*

LIFESTYLE CHANGES

A third application is to be found in the *ba'al teshuva* world (*ba'al teshuva* describes a person who has discovered a Torah-oriented way of life after living a more secular lifestyle). Many *ba'alei teshuva* experience an unexpected and disturbing letdown. First, a young person discovers Torah, becomes inspired by a Torah teacher, and begins to study. Every Torah experience, whether in learning or in contact with the Torah world, is spectacular. Every text studied is alive with significance, every Sabbath experience is high. Somehow though, subtly, this changes and growth has to be sought. Learning may become very difficult. Often the difficulties seem to outweigh the breakthroughs. Many are tempted not to persevere in learning. Of course this is exactly the way it must be, real growth in learning comes when real effort is generated. Just as physical muscle is built only against strenuous resistance, so too spiritual and personality growth is built only against resistance. A person who understands this secret can begin to *enjoy* the phase of work; a maturity of understanding makes clear that the first phase was artificial, it is the second phase which yields real development.

MARRIAGE

Perhaps the sharpest application of this idea in modern society is in marriage. Marriage today is to a large extent in ruins in the secular world. In many communities divorce is more usual than survival of marriage, and even in those marriages which do survive it is common to find much disharmony.

One of the main causes of this disastrous situation is the lack of understanding of our subject. Marriage has two distinct phases: romance, and love. Romance is the initial, heady, illogical swirl of emotion which characterizes a new relationship and it can be extreme. Love is the result of much genuine giving. Love is generated not by what you receive from a partner, but by *giving,* and specifically by giving *yourself.* The phase of romance very soon fades, in fact just as soon as it is grasped it begins to die. A spiritually sensitive person knows that this must be so, but instead of becoming depressed and concerned that you have married the wrong person you should realize that the phase of work, of giving, is just beginning. The phase of building real love can now flourish. In fact, in Hebrew there is no word for "romance" – in its depth it is an illusion.

(We shall look more carefully at this idea in Chapter 11, "Reality and Illusion".)

However, in the world of secular values, the first flash, the "quick fix", is everything. "Love" is translated as "romance" and when it dies, what is left? No-one has taught young people that love and life are about giving and building, and so the tendency is to give up and search for a "quick fix" elsewhere. Of course, the search *must* fail because no new experience will last. Understanding this well can make the difference between marital misery or worse and a lifetime of married happiness. Jewish marriage is carefully crafted to transition from initial inspiration, not to disappointment but to even deeper inspiration.

One of the most important things to understand is the Jewish approach to the intimate side of marriage; in fact there are few things as important. This area is designed to build and maintain inspiration, and it is a subject which must be studied. This must be taught sensitively and modestly; you must seek out an authentic source at the appropriate time and study. Chapter 3, "Man and Woman", is an introduction to this subject.

LIGHTNING IN THE STORM

In all of life, the challenge of the second phase is to remember the first, to remain inspired by that memory and to use it as fuel for constant growth. Remember: life is like a dark night on a stormy plain – lashed by the rain, beaten by the wind, lost in the darkness, you are faced with despair. Suddenly, there is a flash of lightning. For an instant the scene is as clear as day, your direction obvious. But just as soon as it is perceived it disappears; and you must fight on through the storm with only the memory of that flash for guidance. The lightning lasts very briefly; the darkness may seem endless.

That is the pattern of life, short-lived inspiration and long battles. The tools you need are determination, perseverance and a stubborn refusal to despair. Personal ordeals which make despair seem unavoidable are in reality a father's hands, withdrawn so that you can learn to walk. And your work is to remember the flash of light when it seems impossible; that is faith, and that is the measure of who you really are.

BACK TO THE SOURCE

If you remember the phase of inspiration always and use it as your source of energy for battling on into the phase of difficulties, you will return to that level of inspiration; but you will have deserved it and earned it, and therefore you will go far beyond it.

At the end of a lifetime, in the transition from this world to the next, three angels come to greet a person. One of these angels comes to search out: "Where is this person's Torah, and is it complete in his hand?" In other words, have you achieved what you were meant to achieve during your life? The Gaon of Vilna points out, chillingly, that the angel which asks this question is not a stranger. Suddenly one recognizes the very same angel with whom he learned in the womb! And the question to be answered is: Where is that which inspired you then? Where is all the knowledge of the world which we studied together, all the wisdom which was to serve as your inner inspiration to develop yourself and the world to the maximum? Have you brought it into the world and made it real? And can it now be called yours?

Chapter 8

Silence

Τhe culture in which we find ourselves is full of words. The media spew out words constantly. We are surrounded by noise. And yet the only way to develop your true depth is by learning how to be silent.

In a world that is full of talking you have to learn silence. In a world full of noise there is no room for thought, no room for real understanding. You have to develop the skill of finding a quiet place within your own mind in order to get in touch with who you really are. Only in real silence can you really understand. Only one who is silent can really listen.

Only silence can contain deeper knowledge. Let us strive to understand this.

WORDS

Words are limited. Words, no matter how perfectly chosen and eloquent, are fragments of meaning. They are the bits and pieces which communication struggles to construct. If you are sensitive you will know that the deepest experiences are the most difficult to express.

We have a deep need to share the most beautiful and meaningful moments that we experience, and there is a particular pain in being unable to put them into words.

The cure for that pain is to share with someone who has his or her own inner awareness of such things; then words are entirely unnecessary. In fact, the most significant things to be shared in life require no words, demand silence. Words intrude at these times, cheapen the moment.

When you stand silently and witness a scene of deep beauty together with someone close to you, you do not need to talk about what you have shared. You can fully share the moment and its meaning, but not through words. In fact, words would rob the moment of its enchantment, bring it down.

Real communication is possible only with someone who understands you in a way that is deeper than words; someone who has his or her own inner knowledge of that which you experience. When two people have such an understanding, they can communicate. They communicate without words, beyond words. If words are needed, there is probably a lack of communication. And if many words are needed, the attempt is probably hopeless. If you must explain your experience to someone at great length you will find yourself doubting very much whether that person really understands what you mean. The fewer words you need, the more powerful the communication will be.

WORDS AND LIES

Why is it so difficult to put inner grasp, inner understanding, into words? Why is language inadequate? What is the underlying problem here?

Words can never really convey what you mean. The idea is this: you do not grasp things in words; you do not need words to grasp what you know. In your own mind, you know things *as they are,* not as words express them. Words can describe a thing, but they are not the thing itself. When you know something, *you know the thing itself,* not as words describe it but *as it is.* Words can only talk *about* the thing, they cannot say the thing itself.

Just as you grasp yourself without any need for your name, just as you know who you are with no words necessary, so too you know the things that you really understand. Your name is necessary only for others, not for yourself. You have a rich grasp of your own existence far beyond that which any words or names can express. Knowledge, real knowledge, does not require words. Words are necessary only when you need to communicate your knowledge to others; then you must try to put into words those aspects of the thing that you hope to convey. But no matter how much you try, and no matter how articulate you are, you will never convey *the thing itself* in your words. All you can do is say something about your subject, but you can never put into words all that you grasp, all that you hold in your mind.

That is the problem with words. Your mind is not limited by the physical, it can grasp things that are very high, far above the limits of the finite, material world; but words are finite and limited.

BEYOND WORDS

It is essential to develop the ability to think without words, to really know. Before you begin to find the words to describe things, you must know those things. It is essential to get in touch with that part of your mind that actually *knows* things, not just the part that *talks about* things. We are so bombarded by words and talking that we have lost the ability to think beyond words; most people actually think by talking to themselves – they think by saying something to themselves, listening to the words they have said, replying in words, and all of their thought is nothing more than an inner conversation.

But that is a desperately low level of thinking and understanding! In the depth of your mind you are able to know what a thing really is; do not forget that and settle for a very limited verbal discussion! You have a tool that is able to handle essence, not just descriptions of essence. You have a tool that can handle reality, not just pictures of reality. Do not settle for pictures when you can have the real thing. Do not settle for words when you can have essence. Do not allow your inner world to become a cheap and superficial talk show! Learn to live in a world that thinks it is a talk show, a world that spews out meaningless sounds, that has almost

forgotten that meaning can exist at all, and yet live in reality, at least in the inner world of your own mind.

THE LETTERS SPEAK

The Hebrew alphabet begins ד ג ב א. The first letter א *aleph*, indicates deep knowledge, higher wisdom – its numerical value is one, a clue to the ultimate Oneness. There are many secrets hidden in the *aleph*, but the one to note here is that *it is silent*. Real knowledge has no finite sound, it is intangible, inexpressible. The next three letters, the coming down into the finite, the tangible, are ד ג ב in sequence spelling *beged*, the word for a garment, the outer clothing of the invisible core. But *beged*, a "garment", is also the word for "treachery". The garments may lie, they may cover an identity instead of reveal it, that is their nature. The silent center cannot lie, but its outer layers, those layers which have sound, which speak, may speak treachery.

SPEECHLESS

Moses could not speak well because of this problem. The conventional understanding is that he suffered from a speech defect, an imperfection. But the opposite is true: he could not speak well because of his perfection! He was living in a world of truth, where things are grasped as they are, grasped by a pure mind. Moses knew the essence of things, knew things as they really are, far beyond the level of the words which attempt to describe them. Things grasped thus prophetically, essentially, could never be shrunk into words. *That* is why he could not speak well.

Then, after the *miracle* of the giving of the Torah at Sinai *which was exactly that:* a condensing of the Divine word somehow, miraculously, into the words of Torah, Moshe spoke normally. (As the verse states: "These are the words which *Moses spoke.*") It takes a miracle for higher truth to be spoken here, to "clothe" essence appropriately and not "betray" it.

SECRETS

This is the secret behind the hiddenness of the deeper teachings. The name for such teaching is *sod,* "secret". The uninitiated understand that the word "secret" is used because this wisdom is *kept secret,* no-one will tell you what it is. But this is not so; the word "secret" is used because this wisdom *cannot* be told, it can never be put into words! Even when one *knows* the secret, it remains secret! Real knowledge is always far more than words can express. The world of deeper knowledge is secret in essence. It can be understood, but it can never be spoken. In fact, attempting to speak out things from this dimension is liable to break them.

A CHILD'S SPEECH – GIFT AND SACRIFICE

A most potent illustration of the limiting effect of speech is found in the process of birth. The fetus learns Torah, as we have noted previously. When the unborn child knows all of the Torah in the deepest way and the process of birth begins, an angel strikes him on the mouth and he forgets all that he knew. This is strange: why a blow on the mouth? Surely a blow on the head would be a more appropriate cause of loss of memory? But the inexpressibly beautiful idea being taught here is that the blow on the mouth is the *gift of speech!* A blow, understood deeply, is always a challenge to grow, to develop a new faculty or level, and *on the mouth* because that is the organ of speech. As the child gains the seed of the ability to formulate finite words, he loses the clear, intimate knowledge of the higher wisdom! Not just simultaneously with acquiring the gift of speech, but *because* of the gift of speech – being articulate means being able to shrink things into definite, bounded form; and that is exactly the opposite of being able to expand things into their unlimited essence. And only miracle can reconnect the two; miracle – or the work of intense silence.

PAIN TOO GREAT TO BEAR

When someone experiences a very great pain, it may be extremely difficult for that person to speak about the events which caused that pain or about the pain itself. Very many who survived the European holocaust did not speak about it subsequently. Many children and grandchildren of those survivors will tell you that their parents or grandparents would never speak about their experience.

It is usually understood that their silence is due to the fact that the experience was so painful that the victim does not wish to re-open that area of his or her life because the pain would be too great. To avoid having to re-live the experience and suffer the pain again, they refuse to discuss it. In other words, there is a refusal to re-open that area, a refusal to re-experience the pain. That part of the person's life has been closed and must be kept closed.

But that is not the reason for their silence. There is something much deeper here. The real reason that those people remain silent about their horrific experience is *because it cannot be put into words* – it is too great, too deep for words. No amount of words could ever convey the enormity of what happened; it is beyond human ability to express. The horror transcends human grasp, therefore it cannot be expressed. Those people are not silent because they do not wish to talk about what happened to them and to their world; they are silent because *they cannot talk about it.*

One who went through that experience knows that any amount of talking about it would shrink it to finite proportions, to the proportions of the words used to describe it, and that would be a gross misrepresentation of the depth of the experience itself. Only silence is appropriate; only silence can begin to be the appropriate vessel for that which is inexpressible.

THERAPY

This idea has an opposite expression too: the therapy for one suffering a pain too great to bear is to talk about it! If someone has been through a traumatic experience which is causing ongoing anguish, speaking it out may help. Often, a significant part of the problem is the fact that the experience and its pain seem too great to bear; the person feels overwhelmed by the pain. The sheer enormity of the anguish, the very fact that it seems greater than that which could possibly be survived, is a central part of the suffering. That is exactly why it feels overwhelming. And therefore, if a sensitive listener draws that person into discussing the trauma, if the pain is expressed in words, it may begin to shrink to the proportions of the words. Once it has been spoken out, brought down into the world, the pain lessens.

That which was beyond expression has been expressed; that which was beyond measure has been given at least some semblance of measure, some limits.

SILENCE IN TORAH

When one grasps something deep, the first thing to do is to savor its meaning inwardly. To speak it out to someone else immediately is not the correct thing to do. If you really understand something deep and particularly meaningful and you speak it out immediately, you may lose it! If it is still fresh and new, if it has not yet made total contact with your inner being, if it is still alive with all its inexpressible depth and you put it into words, you are in danger of losing that depth.

Rabbi Simcha Zissel once waited twenty-five years before sharing something with his students because he wanted to be sure that it had made genuine contact with his own mind and consciousness before he dared shrink it into words! He knew that when you give specific words to an idea it shrinks to the dimensions of those words. You must wait until the experience of novelty has settled, until the idea has done its work of affecting the inner being before you dare to speak it out.

SILENCE

Silence develops the deep well of the personality. This is an obligation, not a luxury. There must always be more to your personality than you can express. If you can sum up what you are in a few minutes of talking, you are just that – a few sentences from beginning to end. No matter how much is discovered, revealed, there must be infinitely more. People who describe themselves to you fully during their first conversation with you must be very superficial indeed. A person with whom you can have a deep and meaningful relationship is one who has a depth that cannot be expressed, certainly not in a few minutes of conversation. As you get to know such a person you begin to discover that there is far more to them than you realized at first, and as your relationship deepens you continually discover more. At every level you find more than you knew previously, and the relationship is an endless process of discovery. That is a person who has content! And that is the kind of personal depth to cultivate.

It is fundamental to realize that a person is created unlimited. The essence of a person lies in the unrevealed, deeper dimension; one who lives entirely in the revealed, entirely within the confines of that which can be expressed in a few words has forgotten this basic idea. We do not want our lives to be a superficial script, words to be spoken without inner content. We must strive for the depth, for the meaning, for the unlimited. One who strives for it will discover that depth, the endless realm of the spirit. That is the path of Judaism.

THE BODY REVEALS, THE BODY HIDES

The obligation to ensure that there is always more to your consciousness and your personality than meets the eye: that is your obligation.

There is a most moving and deep Torah illustration of this idea. The verses describe King David bringing the Holy Ark up to Jerusalem, dancing before it in joy and ecstasy. His dancing is described in the most expressive way; David was demonstrating his honor of Hashem by dancing thus in public.

When he approaches his home, his wife Michal, daughter of Saul, objects and chastises him for conducting himself in such unbecoming fashion in public. She accuses him of having been immodestly exposed in the eyes of the maidservants and the people *"k'echad ha'reikim* – like one of the empty fellows"*. David responds sharply by explaining that for Hashem's honor his own is not to be considered; he tells her that he would like to do even more: in the eyes of those same maidservants "I will be even lighter than this", he says. The following verses indicate that because of her improper criticism, Michal had no child until the day of her death, and a close reading of the text indicates that in fact she had a child on the last day of her life, she died in childbirth.

What is the meaning of this exchange? What exactly was Michal's concern? What was David's reply? Why was the consequence so serious? Was she concerned because he revealed himself bodily, physically – perhaps his ankles? His knees? All Torah has unlimited depth; what is beneath the surface here?

There is an insight into this narrative which is exquisite in its revealing of our subject. David was not revealing his ankles; that was not the problem. He was revealing his *neshama,* his soul. Dance is a very powerful expression of internality; there is an idea that one can tell if a man has depth from the way he walks, all the more so from dance. David's dancing revealed so much that Michal felt he had emptied himself entirely, exposed his entire *neshama,* his soul, in those Jerusalem streets (*k'echad ha'reikim* – like one of the *empty* fellows!)

and that is never allowed! There is a deep obligation to retain far more depth than that which one reveals. If all has been revealed, made explicit, where is the connection to the source, to the deep well of spirituality? If you empty yourself completely you retain no connection to your source.

If you express yourself entirely, you are entirely within the world; you have lost your connection to that which is endless.

We can only imagine the intensity of the scene – Michal was a very great woman and she felt she had seen to the very depth of David's *neshama;* his dance must have been an expression of pure spiritual fire.

David's reply is unforgettable: "I shall go further than this" – in other words: "Do you think that what you saw revealed is *all there is?* There is *far more* unrevealed than what you perceived! I have not forgotten that very same obligation of nurturing and building depth which concerns you. But you have misjudged my depth." That is how surely it was hidden! And that is how deep it was!

THE QUIET SELF

Silence. That is the training necessary to develop real knowledge. This discipline is particularly important in a generation that is accustomed to speaking everything out explicitly. Because we live in a culture in which all is explicit, in which everything is put into words to the extent that the words are as cheap as can be, you must take great care to guard your deeper self, your genuine private and sensitive inner being. Learn to think and know before you speak; very often you will discover that speech is impossible, and very often you will discover that speech is unnecessary.

It is essential to build a quiet place in your mind. Even when you are surrounded by noise you should be able to hold a deep silence in your inner world. You must learn to escape the noise of meaningless sounds and words that surround us. But first you must still the inner noise, the inner sounds and voices of meaningless chatter, the constant flood of bits and pieces of superficial static which threatens to drown your sensitive ability to hear and to know.

Before you can speak wisdom, you must be able to hear. And before you can hear, you must be silent. In that absolutely quiet place in your innermost depth, you will find wisdom, and you will find yourself. And there you will come to know that in one moment of that silence is contained more than all the words in the world.

Chapter 9

Faith

I. THE KNOWN

What is faith? What is the Jewish idea of faith? If a non-Jew asked you what faith means to us, could you explain it? What exactly is *emuna*, that fundamental Jewish value which is usually translated as "faith"?

Let us start with the usual idea of faith, or belief, and ask some questions about it.

The world usually understands that faith is personal; in other words, it is a private matter. Belief is subjective, it lives in your mind. You believe because you decide to believe; you believe things that cannot really be proved. The whole idea of "belief" is that it is not provable, not really knowable. The word "belief" means precisely that: you believe only those things that you cannot see or really know; if you know something, you would certainly not say that you "believe" it. If something is out of sight, you must believe in its existence, but if something is visible, present in front of you, you do not "believe" that it exists, you know it. For things that you can demonstrate logically, belief is irrelevant. Belief is blind; in fact they talk about "blind faith".

Now if that is what faith means, we are faced with a problem. If you can never prove that what you believe is true, why should you believe it? You might as well believe anything; if it depends entirely on your personal feeling it really makes no difference what you believe.

And there is no way that one belief can be superior to another: if someone tells you that he believes in something that sounds ridiculous, for example, you cannot argue about the matter because if belief is personal and there is no evidence for what you believe, there is no way to demonstrate that your faith is any better than his.

In other words, you can believe in anything you like (or nothing at all) and that is fine; that is considered faith. There is nothing objective about it and no way of knowing if what you believe exists at all.

The general attitude of the secular world is that faith is exactly this; it is personal, private and rests on no objective provable facts. For those who believe, it is fine. For those who do not, that is also fine. And for those who are believers, whatever they believe must be respected, because matters of faith are personal matters and everyone has the right to his or her own personal beliefs.

They would consider it absurd it you asked for proof that a particular belief is true; matters of faith cannot be proved. You believe because it is meaningful to you; that is all.

On the other hand, if faith is provable, knowable, why call it faith? Why talk about belief when what you believe can be shown? Surely that should be called knowledge?

To put it plainly, if the existence of anything beyond the natural can be proven, then surely "faith" and "belief" are inappropriate terms? If you can prove or experience Hashem's existence, then we should talk only of the process of coming to know that existence. In fact, it would be silly to talk about "believing" in His existence at all. And again, if it could never be proved, then why should you believe it at all? What would compel you to accept something that will always remain up to you to believe with no possibility of ever establishing its truth?

In summary, how can *emuna* ever be meaningful – the existence of Hashem is either definitely knowable, or it is not. If it is knowable with a definite clarity, then *emuna* does not exist; you do not have to believe in that which you know. On the other hand, if Hashem's existence is not knowable objectively, then *emuna* is foolish and arbitrary, no more than a personal emotion, really. So what is *emuna*?

What is the Jewish approach to this matter? Do we say that matters of faith are essentially personal and unprovable, or do we say that they are provable and objective? And if they are provable, why do we talk of faith? Why not talk of knowledge?

KNOWLEDGE

The Jewish answer to this question is that what we call *emuna* has nothing to do with the words "faith" or "belief". We do not speak of "blind faith" or personal, subjective faith. We do not commit ourselves to something that is the product of anyone's imagination. We have not committed ourselves to Hashem throughout history because we decided subjectively and personally that such commitment was a good idea. Our commitment is based on *knowledge* of the clearest and most objective kind. We assert that the object of our "faith" can be *proved and known.*

The Torah understanding is that the existence of Hashem is knowable; one can come to know that He exists quite clearly and objectively. In fact, that clarity of knowledge is exactly what we are seeking in our growth.

One of the goals of development in Torah learning is to come to this knowledge rationally and clearly, and Torah study is therefore a very demanding and rigorous training in objectivity. We do not encourage our students to accept uncritically and thoughtlessly; we encourage them to think powerfully and logically. Torah learning is not an appeal to the emotions, it is a very demanding appeal to the intellect. To study Torah effectively you must be able to ask the most penetrating questions and learn to accept only completely satisfactory answers. Only the highest standards of thought and logic are valid. We are not afraid of questions. On the contrary, asking difficult questions which cut to the root of an issue is the basis of learning.

TWO QUESTIONS

Now if it is true that the knowledge we are seeking can be attained, we are faced with two questions:

Firstly, how does one acquire this knowledge? How do you come to know that which is beyond the physical?

And secondly, as we have already mentioned, why talk about faith? If the higher world of spirit can be known, we should talk of knowledge, not belief. At the very least, those who have reached a clear knowledge of Hashem should have no use for the idea of belief; for them there is nothing left to believe; there is only knowledge. Do we say that for prophets and others who have reached these sublime levels of development there is no *emuna*?

ANSWERS

Let us begin with the first question: how is spiritual knowledge obtained? How do we know that Hashem exists?

We have two avenues of access to this knowledge.

1. Experience

Firstly, we met Him. The Jewish people stood at Sinai and experienced a direct revelation; in fact, the only reason for committing ourselves to Hashem is the fact that we had a direct experience of Him; no prophet's testimony would be good enough for us if we had not begun with the most direct and immediate kind of experience. Only because we personally lived through that meeting are we prepared to accept the words of the prophets who spoke later in history.

The Jewish people are by nature a sceptical people; only the very highest standard of evidence is good enough for us.

Understanding what happened at Sinai is absolutely fundamental to a grasp of what Judaism is; and it requires much further study. But at the least we should note that it was radically different from any other revelation claimed by any other person or people throughout history.

For example, all Jews of that generation were present and experienced the revelation, millions of people witnessing that event together. It is remarkable that in the history of mankind, no-one else has ever claimed more than one witness to any supposed revelation of the Divine. Every claimed revelation was reported by the individual who said that the Creator had spoken to him and that individual's testimony was accepted by his followers. No-one has ever produced even one additional witness to his experience, whereas we have the testimony of millions of people agreeing on what happened.

BUT I WAS NOT THERE!

For our generation, centuries distant from Sinai, there is an additional issue. How reliable is the transmission to us of the events of Sinai? To what extent can we rely on the accuracy of the handing down of the details? Is it possible that the whole idea is the result of a vague and unreliable chain of transmission through the generations?

Again, this needs careful and detailed study, and we shall not go into it fully here. But a few points are worth considering by way of beginning an investigation into this subject.

One of them is the timespan. How far away are we, in fact, from the events? How many generations have lived from

Sinai until now, how many stages were there in the chain of transmission?

Many people think that we are thousands of generations removed from that moment of revelation, that vast ages stand between us and our forefathers who witnessed it, countless generations. But a quick calculation gives surprising results: we are now approximately three thousand two hundred years after the event. If we consider a generation to be forty years, a reasonable time for parents to transmit the information to their children, we find that we are only eighty generations away from that time ($80 \times 40 = 3,200$). This is far less than we tend to imagine; a relatively small gap in time. Not that many generations stand between Sinai and us.

And we know who they were. We know who the individuals in each of those generations were; we know their greatness by historical account and we have their original works. We can pinpoint the handing over of the tradition from one great Torah authority to the next, a thread running through time which can be microscopically examined. This is no vague tale stretching back into the mists of time beyond human memory. It is a concrete, crystallized, detailed account which meets the highest standards of accuracy; preserved and transmitted intact over the span of generations by the entire Jewish people.

In addition, we have no record of any disagreement. We have no record of anyone claiming that the Sinai revelation never occurred or was in any way falsified. In fact, not only our records agree – even those who have attacked us throughout the generations accept it; their own religions are openly based on it. While they may disagree (often violently) with each other, they all agree that what we claim actually happened as we claim it did.

Furthermore, it is hard to see how such an event could have been falsified: we would have to assume that somewhere in history a generation of Jews accepted a completely false tale and handed it down to their children with no-one disagreeing or lacking any of the details. At the Passover *seder* which Jews have celebrated since the Exodus itself the story of that Exodus and the Sinai Revelation have been recounted by parents to their children in exactly the same form; no-one suggests otherwise. How did this happen if it is all a wild imaginary tale? How did Jews all over the world propagate exactly the same account throughout every generation with perfect accuracy and agreement on all the details if someone concocted it at some point in time and somehow tried to spread the false story to all Jews? It is very difficult to propose a mechanism which would account for the nature of this transmission if it began somewhere as a lie.

In summary, the first (and more important) avenue of access to knowledge of Hashem is the personal experience of the Jewish people – the Sinai revelation and its transmission to us by each generation of Jews since then.

2. Science

The second method of gaining knowledge of Hashem's existence is through scientific enquiry.

A logical examination of the universe suggests that a higher intelligence has designed and constructed it. There are classic Jewish sources which present this approach and they should be studied; however, you should note that proofs which use this line of thinking are always proofs by exclusion. That is, they prove that the world must have a Creator because the alternative is illogical – to suggest that the universe is a random accident is not logical. The more that is discovered about the universe, the more its incredible fine-tuning and organization are apparent; it is very difficult to understand that all of the world's exquisitely detailed structure is accidental.

Now a proof by exclusion is just as solid as a proof by derivation, but it lacks something: when you derive knowledge of something, you understand it. However, when you prove something by showing that the alternatives are impossible, you may have proved it, but you do not understand it at all. You know it must be true because there is no other option, but you have no direct knowledge of what it is.

When we prove that the world must have a higher source, we can prove it only by showing that the alternatives make no sense; but what that Source is, we do not understand. For that, we need Torah.

Scientific enquiry can take you to the border, to the edge of the physical world. At that border, it is apparent that something lies beyond, but what that something is requires other tools to discover. Using science, you can show that there is a zone beyond science, but to enter that zone you need Torah. That is why our main avenue of access to the knowledge we seek is Torah study. We use science to take us to the border and to show that there is a beyond; we learn Torah to enter that beyond.

REAL FAITH

Now we come to our second question: if we say that proof exists for that which cannot be seen directly, what is faith? If the Jewish people *know* Hashem, as we have discussed above, what is left to believe? Why talk of *emuna* if we really mean knowledge?

The answer is that *emuna* does not mean faith. Faith or belief as these ideas are understood in the modern culture have nothing to do with *emuna*.

The correct translation of *emuna* is not faith but *faithfulness* or loyalty. The concept is this: when you have acquired the spiritual knowledge, when you know clearly that what meets the eye is not all that there is, when you know that Hashem exists and you know what He expects of you, the question then is: *will you be loyal to that knowledge?* Will you live up to it? Will you fulfill your obligations? The problem of *emuna* is not how to gain the knowledge of the spiritual world, it is the challenge of being faithful to that world and its obligations.

"Emuna" derives from the same root as *"ne'eman"*, meaning faithful or loyal. Even the most superficial examination of the use of this word in Torah will show that it cannot be translated as faith in the sense of belief – for example, the verse states *"Va'yehi yadav emuna ad ba hashamesh* – And his hands were loyal until the sun went down"; his hands stayed where they were, they remained *loyal* to their task. The verse cannot be translated in any other way – hands cannot have "faith" or "believe" anything.

Or the verses which describe Hashem speaking to Abraham and then state: *"V'he'emin baShem..."* You cannot translate this verse as "And he (Abraham) believed in Hashem"; it is quite clear that he had been speaking to Him – there cannot be praise for someone who believes in something that he has personally seen and experienced! No, the idea is not that Abraham believed; a prophet does not believe, he knows. The praise here is that he was *loyal*, he stood strong and went through the most difficult tests and ordeals; that is appropriate praise.

A unique feature of being human is that you can know something with total clarity and yet act completely against that knowledge. You can acknowledge that a certain action is wrong and then do it anyway. Free will means that you can act in disharmony with your intellect. Understanding something and all its consequences clearly does not guarantee that you will live in accord with your understanding, that you will be loyal to it. Not at all. It takes work to live up to your knowledge of the truth. And that is the work of *emuna*.

II. THE UNKNOWN

The nature of an ordeal is that even when it begins with a clear obligation to act in a certain way, great strength and courage may be required to carry out that course of action. You know what is right, you know what you have to do, but it may be enormously difficult to actually do it. Will you go through with it? Will you live up to your ideals? That is the test.

Knowing what to do is one problem; but even when you know what to do the difficulty is not over: that is when the test of *emuna* begins – will you have the courage to *do* what you should? Will you have *emuna*, fierce loyalty to that which is right and true?

When Abraham is commanded to leave his home and go on a journey, he is not told the destination. "Go from your land, from your birthplace and from your father's house to the land *which I shall show you*." This is the classical structure of a test. The point of departure is clear; there is no doubt that he must go. The test is that the journey leads into the unknown; what he will find and what he must go through on this journey are not clear at all. The destination will become clear only when he gets there; the entire journey must be made only on the strength of the command to travel.

And this is where we meet the element of the unknown in ordeals. If there is a blindness in tests, this is it. The destination is always hidden; you can never know what the end of the road will be until you are there *because the end of the road is really the greater form of yourself which the test is building.* The purpose of your ordeals is to give you the opportunity to become what you must be; you will know the meaning of that only when you have made it real.

Abraham's journey is towards himself. He must walk the path that leads to a revelation of all that he can become and more than that. He must leave who he is now and go towards the greater man he has the potential to be; and we must all walk that road. To see the result while yet in motion is impossible; if you were shown the result before you had worked to reach it, you would see only a shrunken and distorted version of that result because you are not yet developed enough to be able to see the higher level.

If you are trapped inside a glass prism, no matter how much white light is shone upon the prism you will always see the colors of the spectrum individually. Shining more light onto the prism will not help, you will not be able to see it – *until you break the prism.* Only when the limits of your present situation are shattered will you be able to see beyond those limits.

First you must be prepared to move beyond your present level; only then will you be able to see that which is new. The person of faith, real faith in Jewish terms, is prepared to follow wherever the road of truth leads, no matter how difficult that road and no matter how unclear the destination. The spiritual path demands a commitment to walk that road without the comfortable assurance of knowing where it leads. *That* is faith.

You may hear the person of religious commitment insulted by the secular world; often the criticism is that the follower of the spiritual path, the religious individual, is a blind follower, a mindless ritualist following guidelines unthinkingly. Religion is a "crutch" for weak-minded people, you may hear. But remember that exactly the opposite is true; the path of Judaism requires fearless commitment to higher values, fearless commitment to walk the difficult and often lonely road of the truth with no preconception of what the destination will be. This is exactly the opposite of performing mindless rituals that present no challenge.

ANSWERING THE SCEPTIC

In fact, it is important to realize that the totally secular person, the one who is convinced that the religious path is not for him, is the really narrow individual. Such a person may tell you that he rejects religion because it is narrow and limited, that he is broadminded and follows wherever the truth may lead with no limits, but a little thought will show you the falsehood of his position.

If he has negated the spiritual option before he begins, how broadminded is he really? Sure, he is prepared to follow where the truth leads, *but only within the bounds which he has already defined.* He has decided that there can be nothing beyond the physical, the material; he has limited his possibilities to the world of the natural, and yet he claims to be totally open!

He has set himself completely safe boundaries, he has defined reality very narrowly, and yet fails to see that. He feels that all possibilities are open but he has forgotten that he began by choosing which possibilities exist in the first place. That is not broadminded; that is deliberate blindness.

No; the real seeker for the truth has no limits at all. There can be no defining, no experience of the destination before the journey begins.

OUR JOURNEY

And that is the story of the Jewish people. Ever since that journey began, ever since Abraham stepped out on that long, lonely road to an unknown destination, we have been walking. Always walking, always moving forward through the trials of a great and historic journey. Through fire and water, through exile and brutal adversity, through a history of pain and torture, through a history of cosmic rises and falls, we have been walking.

Loyalty to the journey, a tenacious determination to get to the destination, that is what is required. A fierce loyalty that will not be shaken. That is faith.

DOUBT

In our generation, we have an added problem. Very often, perhaps more often than not, we are not sure what the test is. In other words, what the obligation really is may be very unclear to us. We no longer hear prophetic instructions telling us what to do. Very often we feel that if only we knew exactly what was required of us, finding the strength to do it would be no problem. Our real problem is doubt.

If only you knew exactly what you are supposed to be doing, exactly what Hashem wants from you, you feel you would be able to do almost anything. That was not the problem of the generations of prophecy, but it is our problem.

Our approach to this problem is to gain the greatest clarity that we can. We do not enter ordeals unless we are sure that the course of action we are taking *makes the most sense possible*. We must strive for the wisdom to make clear, logical decisions before we act. We base our actions and general course in life on the well-established precedents of Jewish history; we follow the lead of the great Torah sages whose wisdom and character have been proved time and again. You need a personal teacher who is more mature and objective than you; you need to be sure that whatever you do is based on the best advice and is the most sensible option possible. We do not have prophecy; we must rely on wisdom.

But once you know which action makes the most sense in any situation, once you have done your best to clarify which option you should choose and the decision is made, then you must fight with all your might to succeed in the action or direction you have chosen. Then you must remain loyal to the path you have chosen; once you have the best and clearest knowledge you can achieve, your test is to live up to it.

Chapter 10

Jew, non-Jew and Intermarriage

In the process of defining who you are by looking carefully at your unique personality features, you have to give serious thought to the fact that you are Jewish. What exactly does this mean? What is the difference between Jew and non-Jew? How important is this to your process of self-discovery and self-fulfillment?

It is a feature of our generation that we have lost the natural awareness of the difference between Jew and non-Jew. It is hard for young people to understand how strong this sensitivity was only a short time ago. Many Jews of the previous generation, despite not being observant, had a strong feeling of their identity as Jews. Yet many Jews of this generation hardly relate to their Jewish identity at all. What has happened?

The Talmud states: "Every seventy years a star rises that misguides the ships' navigators." Each generation in Jewish history is tested by a particular mistaken philosophy or ideology. Great ideological movements which are contrary to authentic Jewish values sweep through the world and the Jewish people; each generation is tested and tempted by one of these. Many succumb; many fail to demonstrate the fierce loyalty necessary to stand firm in the face of a new and apparently redeeming approach to life. And seventy years later, the idol crashes and a new one arises; again a generation is tempted and again casualties abound.

The opinion of the greatest Jewish minds of the last generation was that the test of that generation was the communist and socialist idea; in fact many Jews were swept away by its promise of a perfect society. And seventy years after its grand entrance, it crashed and exited the stage of human ideology, one more in a long series of human ideas intended to build a universal messianic reality that have failed.

But what is the ordeal of our generation? What star misguides those who would navigate a course through our part of history? What misperception tests and tempts the minds of Jews today?

It is the blurring of the distinction between Jew and non-Jew.

In the modern Jewish mind, a transition has taken place to a universal grasp of man without distinctions, at least with regard to Jewish identity. The unique nature of the Jewish people and its unique path through history are becoming blurred in the minds of modern Jews. The special beauty and greatness of our people, a sense of the miracle of our existence despite the concerted efforts of vast sections of humanity to destroy us throughout history; the sharp awareness of these things is being lost. Young Jews of this age see an awareness of Jewish identity as irrelevant or negative. At the center of their personal sense of identity is nothing specifically Jewish. A generation ago the center of the Jewish personality was Judaism most definitely and powerfully; today all that remains is a vague and often uncomfortable haze.

The natural pride in that deepest element of the sense of self that has always lived in the heart of a Jew, that natural pride in being a child of Jewish history, is being lost. It is fundamental to understand that *this is unnatural;* the star that rises and misguides the navigators is *unnaturally* placed, it does not belong in that part of the firmament. It is a special distortion, out of keeping with the rest of the natural scene. That intelligent young Jews should regard their Jewishness as irrelevant, unworthy of even the most cursory examination, unworthy of even a passing thought before being cast onto the waste heap of human experience, is nothing short of miraculous.

You must understand this. For an idea and a people that has been at the forefront of human consciousness and events for millennia, that has been at the focal point of world history more than anything else throughout the ages of human activity and conflict to pass out of the consciousness of its sons and daughters to the extent that they are prepared to give it up without even engaging it superficially is remarkable. It is a special test, a test of unconsciousness. The Jewish mind is asleep, drugged by this unusual and unprecedented ordeal. The young and aggressive Jewish mind, that sharp and inquiring mind that has examined and penetrated, discovered, conceived and invented in all areas of knowledge, has lost knowledge of itself. Worse; its has lost even the desire to know itself. The Jewish mind is almost comatose.

The distinction that is natural to the non-Jewish mind is fading from the Jewish mind. The non-Jewish world's sense of the difference between Jew and non-Jew is far clearer than ours; in fact it is a Jewish teaching that anti-Semitism exists to remind us forcibly of our Jewish identity when our own inner sense of who we are fades.

So we are going through a phase in our history in which our picture of ourselves is unclear. Often, the blurring of the picture can be dated accurately: in many families one generation ago things were clear and in this generation they have broken down.

A specific true example will help to clarify this. In a particular family in a certain large city, the parents raised their first daughter with very little Jewishness.

She was sent to a non-Jewish public school despite the fact that they lived near a Jewish school. Their home lacked virtually all Jewish observance and education. The girl had non-Jewish friends and when she grew older, dated non-Jewish boys.

When she was just over twenty years old she married a non-Jew. That is not surprising; what is surprising is her father's response: *he disowned her.* He did not attend her wedding, did not speak to or see her for years afterwards, and refused to see his new grandson.

Now we need to ask what happened here. How can a man give his daughter no Jewish information or education, allow her to grow up in the close company of non-Jews, date non-Jewish young men, and then react so strongly when the obvious and predictable result occurs? How in fact could he expect her to do anything other than what she did?

The answer is clear. That father felt the difference between himself as a Jew and his non-Jewish associates and friends sharply. Marriage to a non-Jew was inconceivable to him. Jewish observance and education seemed irrelevant to this issue; Jews and non-Jews are different and there is no way that they can marry. Quite simply, Jews do not marry non-Jews. He did not consider Jewish education necessary to teach this point; he felt it to be a natural part of a Jew's consciousness.

But his daughter does not see it that way. It is not a natural part of her consciousness at all. She has not been taught to understand that difference and she is not part of a generation that felt it naturally. She does not see her Jewishness as anything more than a cultural fact; she does not feel different from any non-Jew. She thinks that her father is insane; she cannot fathom his inconsistency – to give her no Jewish education and then disown her for marrying a non-Jew is totally unintelligible to her.

And he thinks that she is a traitor; he feels that she has betrayed her family and her people. He cannot understand how she could turn her back on her people and her history. Although he has very little knowledge of what Judaism really is, it is important to him; it is central to his sense of who he is. He cannot imagine a Jew to whom Jewish identity is irrelevant.

He is filled with pain because of what she has done. In his mind he carries indelible images of Jews living as Jews over the centuries, dying in unspeakable pain because they were Jews, suffering indescribable horrors so that Judaism would survive, so that Jewish children would be born who would continue the chain of Jewish survival. He is old enough to remember the destruction of European Jewry in this era; he lived through it and had its message of Jewish identity burned into his consciousness permanently, irreversibly. He grew up in a world in which Jews had no place of escape. He grew up in a world in which non-Jews had reminded Jews about their Jewish identity with unforgettable clarity. Even if he would have liked to forget that Jew and non-Jew are different, the non-Jews had not forgotten, and he had learned that you cannot forget, you dare not forget. He had learned that the Jewish people continue, and that we shall go through whatever is necessary to continue, to bring future generations of Jews into being.

He knows that since we began as a people nothing has been more important to us than this; and his daughter has walked away from it without a thought. To him, that is desperately wrong; that is a betrayal of history and a betrayal of the very heroism and suffering that brought her into existence as a Jewish child in the first place. And he does not see that authentic Jewish education is the key to passing on a sense of the greatness and timelessness of Judaism and the Jewish people; he assumes that those things are passed on automatically.

But they are not passed on automatically. A generation that has grown up without feeling the searing pain of the lessons of former years, grown up with no real distinction between Jew and non-Jew felt in the flesh, such a generation does not understand. That father and daughter cannot understand each other at all.

For those who do not have a natural sense of their own Jewishness, this is an area that needs study. Before walking away from centuries of history, centuries of inhuman suffering and superhuman survival, centuries of Jews who lived and died so that the miracle of this people's survival continues, it makes sense to investigate what this heritage means. The most basic level of honesty and loyalty demands that investigation. You must be callous and unfeeling indeed to turn your back on your people without a thought.

One who intermarries, one who leaves the brotherhood of his people without investigating the nature of that step is a hard brother indeed.

LOST IDEALS

What is the ideology sweeping mankind in general in this generation that provides the backdrop for our loss of identity? What is happening in the minds of our contemporaries in world culture at large that parallels the movement of Jewish minds away from recognition of our uniqueness? It should be plain to you that it is the teaching that men are not different from animals. Man is, in fact, an animal according to the present worldview.

Humans are failing to distinguish themselves from animals. The awareness of humans as utterly different from animals is weak, and Jews are losing their grasp of themselves as unique. After all, if you must battle just to remain human, if you have to justify any higher awareness at all, if your idealism and noble thoughts are explained as animal instincts no different than accidental products of the jungle, how relevant can a unique Jewish identity be? What could be the meaning of Jewish identity and values if we have no real free choice anyway? What could be the meaning of a unique peoplehood if humans are really only biological organisms?

Blurring of the distinction between man and animal; that is the problem in society in general. Blurring of the distinction between Jew and non-Jew; that is ours.

For the first time in history the ideology of the world is that there is no ideology. For the first time in Jewish history the consciousness of a generation of Jews does not include Judaism. Man has lost his inner grasp of himself as man; Jews have lost their inner grasp of themselves as Jews.

THE MERIT OF A PEOPLE

In our sources there is a description of the entrance to the dimension of suffering in the next world. The meaning of that suffering is simply that the soul must experience the pain that it caused in the world; it enters that dimension to experience that pain. The pain is exactly in proportion to the damage that was caused during life; all suffering in the next world is exactly measure for measure. In depth, the pain is nothing other than the deep experience of the damage itself – the soul feels there the harm it has caused itself.

Now that is logical; however there is one feature of the scene that does not seem to be. At that fearful and fateful gateway sits our forefather Abraham, and we have a tradition which states clearly that he pulls out every Jew who is about to enter, except a Jew who has engaged in an intimate male-female relationship with a non-Jew (or otherwise deliberately broken our unique covenant). Such a Jew is not recognized by Abraham, and he is not rescued.

What does this mean? How can one person save another from punishment? How can Abraham prevent a Jew from entering that dimension of justice if that is what justice demands? If that Jew deserves to enter there, where is the justice in pulling him out?

The answer is this. The individual who is about to enter that dimension of deserved pain is a great-grandchild of Abraham. The individual certainly deserves to enter; there are no mistakes or injustices in the world of truth. If that is where he has been sent, that is where he deserves to be.

But Abraham does not deserve it! That heroic and cosmically great forefather of the Jewish people does not deserve to see his grandchild suffer. The grandchild may deserve it, *but the grandfather does not.* That grandfather gave his life for Hashem, he lived only for Him and he achieved a closeness with the Creator that gives him enormous credit in the spiritual world. And that credit extends to his grandchildren because they are his grandchildren.

Imagine a scruffy and unkempt young fellow with an unsavory history who wants to join a very select and elite club which accepts only the very best. The officers of the club eject him unceremoniously without even considering his application. But as they are about to throw him out, he mentions his name: he is a grandson of the founder of the club. That changes things rapidly – they usher him into the inner chambers of the club and serve him a drink.

Why? Because his grandfather started the club. The existence of the entire club is due to this youngster's grandfather; without him they would not be here at all. The youngster does not deserve admission, but his grandfather's merit covers him. The grandfather has such a credit balance, as it were, that his grandchild merits admission. The youngster rides on the merit of his grandfather. The officers of the club owe the young man nothing, but they owe his grandfather everything. When they admit the youngster they are expressing their relationship with the grandfather, not the grandson. They cannot reject a grandson of the founder.

The young man has nothing of his own that can gain his admission to the club; the only merit he has is that he is a grandson of the founder. But that is enough.

When a Jew is about to suffer deservedly in the next world, when no merit of his own can save him, the merit of his grandfather Abraham can. Not because the grandson is deserving at all; he is not. But the grandfather is. That grandfather will suffer when the grandchild suffers because such is the love of parents and grandparents for their offspring. And if the grandfather does not deserve to suffer, the grandchild will be spared because *that* is justice.

Just as you would exert yourself for the child of your close friend out of loyalty to your friend simply because he is your friend's child even if that child were not deserving of your special effort, so Hashem shows kindness to the grandchild of Abraham because he is a grandchild.

All it takes is that the grandchild is in fact a grandchild. He needs no other merit. As long as he is part of a chain that stretches back to Abraham, that is enough.

But if he has broken that chain, if he has taken himself out of the chain of generations that link him with Abraham, he is not recognized as a grandchild. If all he has is his identity as a link in the chain, if all he has left is the fact that he is the product of generations of Jews who married Jews so that he could be born part of that historic chain, *and he takes himself out of that,* what is left?

He is recognized as a grandchild if he remains part of the family; no matter what his conduct he is still a grandchild. But if he destroys his link with the family, if he breaks that one connection he has with his grandfather, what identifies him as a grandchild? After all, you need *something* to rescue you, *some* merit. Even if you have none of your own, the merit of your grandfather Abraham is enough; *but you must be recognizable as a grandchild.* At least that.

And Abraham cannot recognize a Jew who breaks that covenant of loyalty, the covenant of using the intimate marriage bond to link ourselves throughout history. That covenant, the circumcision that Abraham began as the point of origin of the chain of the Jewish people has been maintained unbroken to produce this Jew; and he is now using it to bond outside of the Jewish people – that breaks the chain; that deprives him of the only thing he has left as a Jew. And he becomes unrecognizable.

Chapter 11

Reality and Illusion

When we wish to compare the Torah approach to life with that of the culture in which we live, a most illuminating tool is language. In Torah, words mean what they say. In fact, the words of Torah *are* the very things they describe. Let us study this remarkable idea and then apply it to the values of Torah and culture.

The world was created by means of the Torah. Hashem "looked into the Torah and created the world." The Torah was written before the world was created; it is the plan from which the world is built just as a building is constructed from the architect's plans. Or perhaps, just as the genes code for the features of the body, the words of Torah code for the objects they describe. A word of Torah is the root of an object in the world.

Hashem created the world by saying the words of Torah; each word condensed, crystallized, concretized into the object it formed, and *that is why objects in the world are exactly as the Torah describes them.*

Consider a film projected on a screen. Light shines through the film and is projected on the screen. Whatever is on the film will be projected on the screen; whatever is visible on the screen must have been present on the film. Nothing can appear on the screen if it is not on the film; the images on the screen are faithful reproductions of the film. The Torah is the film; the world is the screen. Everything in the world is a projection of Torah; everything in the world must have its origin in Torah. Torah and the world parallel each other exactly.

CAUSE AND EFFECT

However, the nature of this parallel is often seriously misunderstood. The nature of the parallel between Torah and physical reality is that *Torah is the cause and the world is the result.* It is not enough to understand that there is a correspondence between every detail of the physical universe and the Torah; it is essential to realize that each detail of the world exists *because* the Torah says so. In fact, every fine detail exists exactly as it does in the world only because the Torah itself contains each of those details.

Torah does not describe reality, it is the *cause* of reality.

Certainly, the genetic code corresponds to the physical features of the organism, but it would be a serious mistake to imagine that the genes somehow reflect the physical reality in coded form; the genes do not reflect – they are the *reason* that the body looks as it does, they are the instructions and the mechanism which construct the body. In fact, the body is a reflection of the genes!

The Torah is the genetic material of the world. The words of Torah are Hashem's words; but His word is not simply spoken by Him while He creates the world by some other means; His word *is the means, the mechanism of Creation.* Each word spoken by Hashem in creating the world *becomes* the object it describes.

In Hebrew, unlike other languages, the word for a "word" and the word for an "object" are the same: *"davar"*. Why? Why do we express two concepts by means of one word? The reason is that they are, in fact, one: every object in the world is a word of Torah! That is exactly what it is. Other languages are conventions, their words mean what they say only by agreement, there is nothing intrinsic in the words that means what they describe. In Hebrew, the language of creation, words mean exactly what they describe *because they are the things themselves.*

TORAH MISUNDERSTOOD

This idea is particularly difficult to grasp in the modern era. Western thought is firmly based in the finite, physical dimensions; the yardstick of reality is the laboratory, and that which is not tangible or measurable by experiment is not taken seriously. At center stage in this grasp of the world is the fact of physical existence; spiritual wisdom is seen, at best, as commentary.

The result of this worldview when applied to Torah is the idea that Torah describes, analyses, comments. One often hears admiring statements about Torah flowing from this perspective – how deep the Torah is, how penetratingly it perceives all aspects of the world. But in reality this is nonsense and one who speaks thus speaks against Torah.

To make this point clearer, let us consider a typical example. You will probably hear it said that the idea behind the laws of kosher food is health – certain foods are not kosher because they are unhealthy. The Torah, in its great wisdom, prohibits such foods in order to safeguard the health of those who heed its commands. Some types of meat are prone to tapeworm infestation; shellfish inhabit parts of the seabed which are contaminated with hepatitis virus and other pathogens, and so on.

Of course there is truth in this approach – Torah living *is* healthy; a major benefit of the Torah-observant way of life is physical and mental well-being. But a moment's thought will show the fundamental error of one who takes this view: *such a person understands the physical world to be primary*, the world is the way it is as a primary fact – some foods are unhealthy, some are not; that is simply the way things are. And now, *after the fact*, the Torah deals with that reality: eat this food, do not eat that. The Torah is secondary to a finite world, and of course it too must be finite. The absolutely inevitable next step is: of course, the Torah must be subject to change! Previously unkosher foods which are no longer unhealthy due to modern inventions or improvements can now be eaten! After all, the entire basis for the prohibition was a health consideration!

But the spiritual secret is exactly the opposite. Certain foods are forbidden; the reason is *entirely spiritual*, whether we grasp some of that spiritual depth or not. The *primary* element is the spiritual, the transcendent. That comes first. In fact, it could be that the physical attributes of the forbidden food are as they are *because* the spiritual essence is impure: the shellfish inhabits its contaminated habitat and may be physically unhealthy *because it is unkosher!*

Torah comes first; the world follows. Torah is the cause; the world is the result. This is the grasp which a Jew should have. One who wishes to become spiritually conscious must make an effort to break the patterns of Western thought which bind the world within finite boundaries. The higher wisdom must be primary.

The secularized modern view breaks all of Torah into fragments of finite proportion. The Sabbath is perceived as a day of rest in the sense of physical rest; its prohibitions are those of work in the sense of physical exertion. And of course, we can do as we please with those prohibitions because times have changed – what was work in earlier times is no longer work! Lighting a fire was once a tiring procedure and that is why it was forbidden; today it is done with a flick of the wrist and so it must be permitted!

And again, the truth is entirely different. The observance of the Sabbath is a *spiritual* matter; the idea of physical rest is very much secondary. In fact, there is no Torah prohibition of physical exertion at all. Lighting a flame is a creative act and that is the essential element, the degree of physical exertion is *irrelevant*. And lighting a flame today is every bit as creative as it ever was. But secular eyes see a finite world, and in that view all of spirituality is reduced to the very limited dimensions of the material.

WORDS – REAL AND UNREAL

In Torah, words always express essence, and close study of the words is rewarded by an understanding of the nature of the ideas which those words describe. In the secular world, words are also revealing: the language of a culture reveals its heart. If one inclines a sensitive ear to the expression of ideas within a society one gains insight into its values.

Now there is a fascinating class of words which exist in the language of the secular culture in which we live which have no equivalent in Torah. There is no translation of these terms into authentic Hebrew – no source is to be found in Scripture. Many of these words represent central ideas within society, and yet they exist only outside of Torah.

What is the meaning of a word which does not exist in Torah, in the language of Creation? The inescapable answer is that, somehow, such words are describing things which are not part of the original Creation, not part of the real world. They do not represent Divine energy which has crystallized into existence; they cannot represent more than the human source which invents them. They may convey concepts which are clear within the context of a culture, but the fact that the language of Creation and essence does not contain them reveals that they convey illusory ideas. They may exist in the imagination of people, they may describe and motivate human behavior and action, but they are essentially of human manufacture. Words that are not found in Torah describe illusions.

If something appears on the screen which is not on the film, someone must have painted that thing up on the screen; it was not part of the original source. The film projects itself faithfully onto the screen; but this detail has been added later, it has been laid over the authentic picture. It may appear like all the other details in the picture, but it is not authentic. And only by examining the film itself will you discover which details are authentic and which are superficial additions.

Before we look at words in the secular world, however, you should note that within the Torah tradition itself we find words which have no Scriptural source but were coined by the Sages – such words describe concepts which are clear to the human mind but have no absolute or objective basis. Examples of such words are *safek*, meaning "doubt" (and also *vadai*, meaning "certain") and *teva*, meaning "Nature".

Consider these for a moment.

DOUBT: Doubt is not an objective creation – nothing was created "doubtfully"! Things either are or they are not; it is the subjective human experience of uncertainty which is described by the word "doubt" and that experience is purely human, not Divinely objective. (Of course certainty, too, is not an objective Torah idea; if there can be no doubt in the absolute sense, then there can be no certainty either – when things exist in the real world, they do not *certainly* exist, they simply exist. Certainty is an idea which is relevant only where doubt is a possibility.)

So doubt was never created, it is not real outside of our minds. Therefore the word which conveys this experience of confusion was devised, invented, by the Sages; it is a human concept. We experience it, so we need to name it, but in truth it is an illusion.

NATURE: Nature, in the sense of an independent, self-generating and self-maintaining system, is illusory. The fact that the world appears to function on its own, without obvious control from any higher Source, is certainly a human perception, and that perception is contained in the word "Nature", but the Torah does not contain such a word. The correct understanding is that there is no "Nature", no independent self-contained system that functions of its own accord. In reality, there is only Hashem; nature is no more than an emanation of His being. In essence, the appearance of independence is inaccurate.

NO WORDS

There are other words, too, which are absent from the Torah. In Hebrew you cannot say "I have"; there is no word for this. There is no word at all, not even one of Rabbinic origin. The reason for this is that in a materialistic culture, value is material: how much a person is worth depends on how much that person *has*, or owns. Your value is reflected in your possessions, you are rich if you have much. In Torah, value is not material; your value depends on what you *are*, not what you have.

Torah does not confuse essence with possession; the language of Torah grasps the essence and existence of things as primary, not their material value. In Hebrew, when you wish to say that you own something you cannot say "I have it"; you must say *"Yesh li ... "*, which means *"It is* to me", that is, *"It exists* in relationship to me"! The language forces you to express essence; you cannot express false values in the words. *"Yesh"* means *"it is"*, that is how you must begin, by expressing the real existence of the thing; only then can you add the idea that this thing relates to you in some way.

SOCIETY'S WORDS

With this background in mind, it is instructive to search the vocabulary of a society and to identify those words which convey values important to that society but which do not appear in Torah. You may be surprised to find a number of terms which may seem indispensable and central to the thinking of a generation or even an entire culture and yet which have their origin solely in the mind of that generation or culture.

If we were to assemble a list of such terms, we could include Romance, Etiquette, Chivalry, Adventure, Entertainment; and there are many others. Remember that these words convey ideas and values which are integral and important within present society, and remember that in Torah there are no words for any of these. Let us study some of these in order to see whether in fact they fit our definition of ideas which contain illusory elements. We shall find that these ideas and values represent externalities; they exist in the world of physicality and materialism, but in the world of essence, they are illusions.

ROMANCE: Romance is certainly one of the major elements in the culture that surrounds us. Much, if not most, of its literature and entertainment revolves around this experience. What is it exactly?

The heady swirl of emotion experienced at the beginning of a relationship is the hallmark of romance. There is no Hebrew word for this idea; Hebrew certainly has a word for love, *ahava,* which at its core denotes giving. We have already studied aspects of this subject; let us look further.

What is the difference between love and romance? Love is the result of much genuine giving (not of taking, as is the mistaken belief in modern society). Real giving, giving of the self, generates love, and that love is real. You love where you give, not where you take. When you give, and particularly when you give yourself, you love. When you give yourself to someone intensely, totally, you will love that person. Parents always love their children more than children love their parents; the reason is that parents give to their children, they give life itself, and that is how their love comes to be. That is the direction of the giving, and that is the direction of the love.

This is one of the most important things to understand, particularly in an age of self-gratification where love is confused with the good feeling of receiving. When you receive from someone and it makes you feel good, you do not necessarily love that person; on the contrary, if you think about it you will see that what you really love in those situations is yourself! You love what the person does for you, you love the good feeling, in fact, you love yourself. No; real love is where you give, not where you receive.

But romance has nothing to do with giving. It is the experience of newness, the quick infatuation which is generated by superficial appearance, and it is illusory. It lasts only long enough to convince you that it will last forever; in fact that is exactly when it collapses! Of course it has a purpose, and that purpose is to inspire, to begin a relationship with energy and hope. In that sense it is a gift; but relative to genuine love it has no name.

Modern society confuses love with romance. Romance is advertised and sold as love, and of course, when romance dies, as it must, there is nothing left but pain and disillusionment. No-one has taught this generation that real relationships are built by the very hard work of giving, and therefore when the taking begins to wear thin, the relationship dies.

Romance comes at the beginning of a relationship, love comes later. And the height of the romantic notion is "Love at first sight", the clearest contradiction imaginable. Love is not possible at first sight; there has not yet been any giving. First sight reveals only the superficial, and only a superficial illusion of love can result.

ETIQUETTE: Again, we have no word for this. The notion of etiquette comprises the system of rules of proper behavior. Correct behavior is close to the essence of Torah, but the question is: what is the source and the reason behind the behavior – is it the expression of a deep quality of good character, or is it simply superficial action designed for appearances? The element within etiquette which expresses inner character is certainly valid (all superficial and even false ideas and practices contain some truth – that is the reason for their continued survival!); but etiquette comprises mainly rules of conduct which are followed for the sake of the rules, *it is the rules themselves which are important.* Details of behavior and appearance are observed because the rules of etiquette require them. Whether it is the arrangement of silverware on the table or the way a military officer and gentleman drinks his port, these things are essentially outer shows. Many of the practices dictated by etiquette are very important in polite society; one's good breeding and character may be judged by these observances, and yet in essence they are empty.

In Torah, there is no such thing. In Torah, every action is an expression of the deepest wisdom; the action is always an expression of essence *and* an exercise in training good character. In Torah, every fine detail of conduct is an expression of depth and a builder of depth. Nothing is done for outer appearances only, nothing is a superficial show. Our appreciation of character is based on the extent to which behavior reflects real inner quality.

A young man who had recently found his way back to a Torah way of life expressed his confusion to his Rabbi and teacher. He had groomed himself in good manners and gallantry in the secular world and achieved a polished level there, and now he was attempting to learn the Torah's rules of *derech eretz,* good conduct. Should he walk first, or should his wife? Should he open the door of his vehicle for her, or is that a non-Jewish convention which has no place in Torah? And so on. The Rabbi patiently explained: "Conduct yourself with *sechel,* intelligence. Those questions depend on the circumstances: if it is raining, open her door first and let her in. But if it is hot, you enter first and open the windows!" Torah conduct, *derech eretz,* expresses and trains good character; the inner depth must always be in harmony with the outer expression.

ADVENTURE: The thrill of doing things for the sake of doing them, and particularly when danger is involved, is the basis of the world's idea of adventure. As we have noted previously, all problematic concepts have sparks of truth and spirituality within them, and this is no exception – many adventurous activities have aspects of value and beauty. But the search for and preoccupation with dangerous adventure has no place in Torah. What sensible and responsible individual would go out to face danger unnecessarily? Why would anyone throw himself off a cliff with a rubber rope attached to his ankles in order to come as close as possible to annihilation before surviving? What exactly is the drive that leads people to do these things?

The truth is that the motivation for such behavior is the desire to experience life, to feel alive. Think about it: at the peak of a dangerous experience death is very close, then one moment later the danger is over. At that moment, life is felt very richly. *The thrill of facing death and surviving is in fact nothing other than the thrill of life itself.* What pleasure does this person have in the moment of survival? Only the sharp awareness that he is alive; that is all. That is an incredibly sharp pleasure; and the reason is that *life itself is the greatest thrill of all.* But one who has no sense of being alive cannot feel this; one who does not know what life means and what it is worth feels no thrill.

And such a person must throw himself off cliffs in order to experience a few brief seconds of how life feels. He must enter a situation in which life hangs in the balance, in which life seems about to end, so that when it continues he can feel a very brief sensation of that life. You should readily see what a tragedy this is, what a travesty of the idea of life itself.

What a pathetically empty existence it must be that requires approaching death for the sensation of life!

So one who lacks genuine life and growth experiences will seek the thrills of adventure. Of course Torah has no word for this; genuine character growth is the most living experience possible and one fully engaged in it will not feel the need to flirt with death.

Discovering and building the self – that is the real adventure. If you are striving and growing, conquering your own character and building it, you will not need to prove that you are a hero by engaging in the emptiness and the dangers of a world that lacks the thrill of life.

ENTERTAINMENT: The world around us invests much time and energy in this area. Certainly, some forms of entertainment may include elements of value. But if you examine the entertainment of the society around you, you will find that much of it is designed simply to fill time or to provide pleasure by means of imagination or fantasy, very often with immoral or violent material.

This is not new; throughout its history society has enjoyed these things – the theaters, circuses and arenas of the ancient world had much in common with those of today. What is the meaning of viewing immorality and brutality for relaxation or pleasure? Some forms of entertainment involve live cruelty and suffering, even in sophisticated society. Brutality and immorality are condoned by society, and some forms of cruelty are enjoyed specifically by educated and cultured people. What is the nature of a society that *enjoys* these things?

This is not part of Judaism. We should have our hands full with the real aspects of life; who needs to seek ways of killing time? Who would want to seek pleasure in real or imagined experiences of pain or immorality? Who wants to experience horror as entertainment?

And who would want to raise children exposed to every form of immodesty and violence everywhere they look? Who could possibly expect children to develop a refined sensitivity when they are exposed from the very youngest age to the most realistic graphic images of the sort of violence that should turn the stomachs of grown men? Who can expect a gentle and sensitive youth to grow amidst a bombardment of violence, immodesty and shamelessness? How can a young generation work seriously on refining its conscience and developing self-control when its elders spend their time enjoying all the opposites?

REAL WORDS, REAL VALUES

These words are part of the culture around us and many have become part of our minds. But Torah does not contain them. Someone has painted these things on society's screen, but they are not to be found in the source. Someone has painted these things on the screen of the mind, but they do not exist in the pure soul. If you seek wisdom, if you seek real knowledge, you must clear the screen, erase the pictures that are etched onto reality so that the real picture, the real projection of a deeper reality can be accurately seen.

The ideas and values we have examined (and many others dear to modern society) that have no expression in Torah exist on all sides; a thinking and sensitive Jew must examine all of his or her surroundings before accepting any element of the world. Following the ways and habits of society blindly is not a Jewish tradition; Abraham was ready to stand apart from the entire world and so must we. Our tradition begins with the courage to think independently and decide independently; we do not follow the values of the world simply because they are accepted. Even if the world takes on certain values without exception, even if the whole world stands on one side of all the issues, we must have the clear vision and raw courage to stand apart. That is Jewish vision and that is Jewish courage.

Chapter 12

Ordeals

We have studied the idea of free will, the most important aspect of the human being. As we have seen, free will operates in the battle zone of moral ordeals. Let us focus on the subject of ordeals and the personality tools needed to deal with them successfully.

It is a basic Torah idea that a major part of the purpose of life is to stand strong in ordeals. Now an obvious question arises: why would Hashem test us if He knows beforehand what the outcome will be? If ordeals are "tests", as the word *nisayon* is often translated, the purpose of these tests cannot be for

Hashem's learning anything about us, of course. So why does He test us?

We can ask another question too. The word *nisayon,* ordeal, is based on the root *nes* meaning a miracle. The problem is, what do ordeals have to do with miracles? Exactly which element of a test is miraculous?

We can ask this question most sharply like this: when you are faced with a real ordeal, can you overcome it or not? If you can, where is the *miracle* in succeeding? And of course, if you cannot, why would Hashem demand the impossible of you?

We can put this another way. We have said that tests always occur at your point of free choice, that is exactly where you are tested. But we must take a closer look: is a test *at your level* or is it *beyond your level*?

If it is at your level, within your capacity to succeed, then of course you will be able to succeed, and there is nothing miraculous about that. It may take enormous effort, but it will not be miraculous.

If, on the other hand, a test is pitched *beyond* your level, above your point of free choice, at a point which is outside your ability to succeed, then a successful result would indeed be miraculous. But the question then becomes: how can you do it? How can you do the impossible? *How do you perform miracles?*

A CLASSIC ANSWER
One of the answers usually given to our first question, that of why Hashem would test us if He knows the outcome

beforehand, is this: there is an idea that a test forces you to discover levels of your own inner strength which were previously hidden. The difficulty of the test brings out that which would have remained dormant without it. It is not Hashem who discovers what you are capable of when you succeed in a test, it is you! Of course He knew before the test what you were capable of achieving; but *you* did not! *You reveal to yourself* what you are really capable of achieving. You discover the hidden greatness that lies within yourself.

Let us explore this. You have two levels of greatness within: one of which you are aware, and one much higher than you realize. Under normal circumstances, you can reach only the lesser of these, but under the stress of an ordeal, you will reach the higher one. To make this clear, imagine the following experience:

You are standing in an open field. You are practicing leaping over obstacles; you wish to jump as high as possible. After much practice, you discover the highest object you can clear. You try many times, but you cannot leap any higher. No matter how much effort and determination you apply, that is the highest object over which you can jump. Now while you are standing there, gathering your strength for another attempt to better your record, you hear something behind you. You turn and see a large, enraged bull racing across the field directly towards you, nostrils flaring, head down, lethally sharp horns unmistakably aimed at you.

What do you do? You run. You run towards the fence that surrounds the field, seconds ahead of the danger. You sail gracefully over the fence, and drop shaking to the ground on the safe side. As you steady yourself and try to avoid thinking about what would have happened had you been two seconds slower, you notice that the fence over which you leaped so effortlessly *is much higher than the obstacle you had been trying unsuccessfully to clear* before the wild bull appeared. You have far exceeded that which was your limit before.

The reason? When you were trying to jump over obstacles in the field, you were not terrified. But when the bull charged and your life was in danger, you experienced the surge of adrenaline that accompanies mortal terror and your body became capable of much more than it could ever manage under normal circumstances. The pressure of the threat accessed an energy which was previously locked, and you revealed an ability that was previously unknown to you. You discovered your true capability. You discovered that your previous limit was no limit at all.

You discovered, in fact, that there are two limits to your ability to act; one which applies under normal conditions, and one which is hidden until pressure reveals it.

The function of a test is to provide the pressure, the spiritual adrenaline, to force you to discover a level which is far higher than the one you are accustomed to attaining. It brings out your higher self, your true greatness.

Why is this necessary? Why is it necessary to discover and reveal the higher level of your potential, the level which was always there but remained locked within and hidden until the test brought it out?

The reason is that you are here for the purpose of bringing your potential into the actual, for building what you must be from the raw material of your potential. Before the test there was a level of power locked within you which was potential only; after the test that power has become actual, brought into your personality and the world. For Abraham to be *able* to sacrifice his son is not enough – he must make that ability an action, he must bring it into the world. What counts is not what you *can* do, but *what you actually do* in life.

In other words, the reason you are put here in the first place is to become the most that you can become, to achieve all that you can achieve. *The Jewish idea of the purpose of life is to develop yourself to the maximum;* to become the most sensitive, aware, loving, clear-minded and moral person possible. And your ordeals are the means to achieve that: as you battle through your challenges and win, you develop each area of your character and bring your potential into the actual. You become what you must be. And most important of all, *you do it yourself* – you are the cause of your own growth, you build yourself.

This approach is certainly true, and if you understand it well you will find endless motivation for living and achieving. Certainly ordeals are the means for discovering the self. But we have not answered our second question: where is the miracle? If the potential was always present, and was brought to light by the test, that is not miraculous. Great, perhaps. Satisfying and deep, certainly. But not miraculous.

We must look further.

A DEEPER ANSWER

When that enraged bull attacked and you leaped over the fence, you leaped higher than ever before, higher than you would have thought possible, and as we have seen, you discovered a new area of your own possibilities. *But that fence has a limit:* no matter how great the terror, no matter how fierce the bull tearing towards you, there is a fence which you cannot clear. Under pressure, you may clear an amazingly high fence, one which seems superhumanly high, but that has a limit. If the fence were higher than a certain measure, you would not make it under any circumstances, under any pressure.

In other words, there is a limit to your hidden ability too. Your deeper level may be incredibly greater than your usual one, *but it has a limit.* When you amaze yourself and clear that fence you have revealed and attained a great level, *but it is not miraculous.* It is not the impossible which has occurred, only that which perhaps seemed impossible before. So again, why do we refer to ordeals in terms of miracles? A miracle means that which is *impossible under any circumstances.* If a test reveals a miracle, as its name implies, it must mean that in handling the test you leap even higher than your hidden absolute level. Somehow, under the pressure of an ordeal, there must be a way of clearing a fence which is higher than your hidden limit, higher than anything which you could do under any circumstances. What does this mean? How is this to be achieved?

The Talmud gives us a fascinating insight into this problem. In explaining the background to King David's relationship with Batsheva and the sin he committed, the *gemara* records the following conversation between David and the Creator. David asks: "Hashem, why do we say 'God of Abraham, God of Isaac and God of Jacob', but we do not say 'God of David'?"

Let us understand this question. David was certainly not asking in empty pride. He was a true servant of Hashem who had virtually conquered pride entirely; in fact according to the deeper wisdom David represents the power of kingship, which means a revelation of Hashem's rule – the Jewish king is simply the agent who makes the Divine rule apparent in the world. The *mashiach,* the Messiah, is to be descended from David and an extension of his person and soul, and his purpose will be to bring about a recognition of Hashem's rule, certainly not human rule. The attribute of the *mashiach* and Jewish kingship is described as "He has nothing of his own."

(In fact, the name "David" is spelled *daled, vav, daled* – the *daled* is the letter of emptiness, absolute poverty. *"Dal"* in Hebrew means poverty stricken, having nothing. Then comes *vav,* the letter of addition; the *vav* denotes joining, adding, connecting. So David's name means that he begins with poverty, emptiness; he has no content of his own – utter humility. Then he is connected with the source, he is given everything, and yet the last letter of his name is the same as the first: he remains the same simple, humble person he was in the first place.

In contrast, David's cosmic arch-enemy is Gog, the king who will come to battle the *mashiach.* Gog is spelled *gimel, vav, gimel* – the *gimel* means overflowing, having more than necessary. Gog begins as a self-important, overfilled individual. Then he is connected to the source, shown reality clearly, and yet the last letter of his name, too, is the same as the first: he remains the same prideful, self-inflated individual he was before.)

So David was asking in utter humility. David, who so intensely represents the idea of total service of Hashem, wanted to know where he fell short: Abraham, Isaac and Jacob merit to have their names mentioned together with the

Divine Name; in other words, they reveal Hashem's presence by their lives, and David does not. If all four of them are to function together, as they must eventually, David wanted to know what element of his life had not yet been adequately developed. If he is to be the completion of what Abraham, Isaac and Jacob began, it is essential that he fulfill his role. Why do we not say "God of David?" Why is my name not said together with Yours? What have I not yet done in Your service? What am I lacking? What did they do that I have not done?

Hashem answers: "They were tested by Me, and you have not been tested." In other words, the reason that the Jewish people refer to Abraham, Isaac and Jacob in the same breath as Hashem's name is because they went through the fire of tests. Because they were tested and were victorious in their tests, their names are joined with Hashem's.

Immediately David cries: "Grant me a test!" If that is the reason, if I am not what I should be because I have not proved myself in the fierce fire of tests, then test me!

What is the result? He is granted a test, and he fails.

Now there is much here that needs explanation, but the first thing we see is the startling idea that the result of being tested and succeeding is that Hashem's name becomes attached to the name of the one who is tested. What does this mean?

THE ULTIMATE PARTNERSHIP

A name is a revelation of essence. If a person's name, revealing his essence, is spoken together with Hashem's name, the idea is that an aspect of Hashem's presence is revealed in that person; that individual has somehow become a vehicle for His appearing in the world. Somehow, through being tested, the person who handles the test correctly brings Hashem's presence into the world. The individual who lives up to his or her tests becomes a partner in the revelation of a higher reality. When Abraham is tested at the *akeida,* the binding and sacrifice of Isaac, Hashem is revealed. How does this happen?

The answer is this: a real test is *impossible.* It stresses a person beyond all possible limits. The feeling of the enormity of a real ordeal is accurate: *this test is too much for me!* That is correct, it is too much for you! It is more than your utmost effort could achieve.

You cannot do it, but He can. You make the effort, the impossible effort, and He effects the result.

When a person faces the impossible chasm, and leaps anyway because Hashem asks it, and *miraculously* arrives on the other side, Hashem is revealed because only He can do the impossible – *that* is the miracle!

Two elements are required: to attach yourself to Hashem; and then to leap. The Sages tell us that a person's own lower self attacks him daily with lethal viciousness, (the essence of all tests), and "If Hashem does not help, one *cannot* overcome it"! There are no inaccuracies in the statements of the Sages – if they say that without Divine assistance the battle is impossible, so it must be. So to achieve victory in ordeals is to see the Divine hand!

But more than this: to achieve victory in ordeals is to become *the cause* of His appearing in the world! Because you leaped the impossible leap, because you demonstrated your attachment to Him, demonstrated your knowledge that if He wants this leap and commands it He will not let you down *no matter how difficult the ordeal,* He appeared and carried you over.

You would not have been carried over if you had not leaped. The miracle of succeeding in a test, the miracle of climbing to a higher level than was possible for you before, happens only when you make the first move, when you display the courage to do what you must do. When you attach yourself to Him and stay attached *no matter what,* He completes the impossible part of the process and an incredible partnership is formed.

In other words, if you *know* that the test facing you is impossible, that it is greater than you, that there is no way you can win this battle you face, *and then in fact you manage,* the only conclusion you can draw is that Someone must have helped you through! *Your* part in the victory is the action you took: you fearlessly acted despite knowing that the resistance, the enemy, was greater than you. You found the courage to do what you had to do because it was necessary, because it was right, and you ignored your limitations. You relied on the fact that you would not have been asked to do this thing if it was not meant to be. You relied on that which is beyond you, in fact, and *that* is the meaning of faith. You went beyond your own narrow world of self-confident ego, you gave that up, you opened yourself to a dimension greater than your own, and you found a greater version of yourself, greater than you were before and greater even than your secret and hidden level. In short, you have gone beyond the person you were and become someone different.

Clearing fences that are within your hidden limit under extreme pressure may reveal your secret strength, but it does not make you truly different. It cannot create anything truly new, it can only bring out that which lay within already. But a real ordeal does much more; it creates the ability to leap to a level which was literally impossible before, and therefore you become literally new. In fact, if you think about it carefully you will see that this is the only possible mechanism of real growth. If ordeals only brought out the hidden but did not develop that which is beyond the hidden, you would never be able to grow beyond a full revealing of what already lies within. You could hope for an actualizing of your potential, but no more than that. *You would have an absolute limit,* your growth could never exceed your locked-in inner limit.

And the truth is that you are entirely unlimited. Through your ordeals, through the difficulty of your ordeals, *because of the difficulty* of your ordeals, because they are so difficult that they reach into the realm of the impossible, you can achieve the impossible. *There is no limit to what you can achieve.* Each time you are tested, each time you are asked to reach up, to stretch for that impossible dream, you are being invited to shed your limitations. And each time you manage you will be asked to leap higher, and as long as you live you will be asked to leap. And you will bring Hashem's presence into the world. *You* will bring Him into the world. His Name and yours will be said together, partners in building the world.

When a person acts beyond the level of normal, expected human action, Hashem is revealed. The *gemara* records that Shimon ben Shetach, the great scholar and sage, once bought a donkey from a non-Jew and discovered a precious jewel attached to it. He returned the jewel to its owner, explaining that he had paid for a donkey, not a jewel. The non-Jew exclaimed: *"Baruch Elokei Shimon ben Shetach* – Blessed is the God of Shimon ben Shetach!" That response so clearly expresses exactly what we have learned: not "Blessed is Shimon ben Shetach" but "Blessed is *the God of* Shimon ben Shetach" – Hashem's name together with his! The non-Jew appreciated immediately that when a human acts against human nature he is expressing a connection with a higher reality – a small miracle has occurred! No part of the natural world ever goes against its nature, no atom, no molecule, no animal ever goes beyond the bounds of its own possibilities. No animal ever denies its nature in reaching for a higher value; so when the Jew returns an object of great value which he could have kept and enjoyed riches, the intelligent onlooker sees evidence of something higher in the world, sees that there is more than the law of the jungle, the law of blind selfishness. He sees that there is value beyond material value. He sees the uniquely human and he sees, in fact, the Divine.

Luzzatto, author of the classic work of Jewish character building which maps out the path that leads to the supranatural levels that can be attained by correct work on the self, when dealing with those higher levels which a person can reach, says: "The beginning is work, but the end is a gift." The beginning of the path which leads to a higher reality is hard work, very hard work, but the end is a gift, it comes from elsewhere, from beyond the work, beyond the self, beyond the range of the individual.

The Sages say that if a person states that he "labored and found" he is to be believed. Labor will lead to results; but the words are so potently clear: the word *metziah*, "found", connotes an *unexpected* find; it does not say "labored and achieved" but rather "labored and *found*" – the find was unexpected, a surprise *despite* the work because it so completely belongs to another dimension. *What you find when you labor is more than the labor could have produced.*

The prayer of one who stands tested, therefore is: "Hashem, this test that You have given me seems impossible. I cannot humanly overcome it. But if You have seen fit to test me in this way, I shall go through the impossible for You. I shall leap; I give myself to You. I acknowledge that I am nothing, You are everything. Help me through."

APPLICATION

Let us apply this idea. The *akeida,* the binding of Isaac: the impossible test – to sacrifice a son for whom Abraham had waited into extreme old age, from whom he foresaw the Jewish people descending; after teaching the world that human sacrifice is wrong; a man whose entire personality was kindness and love. And not just to harm that son in some minor way, but to kill him with his own hand. And beyond the emotional level, the intellectual level was far more difficult – it made no sense: Hashem had promised him offspring from Isaac – how could there be a contradiction in the Divine? But there is an even deeper problem: Abraham *knew* that Hashem *did not want this sacrifice,* as the verse states: "Which I *never intended."* As one who loves knows the mind of the beloved Abraham knew that Hashem did not, could not, want this act – and he was correct; in fact ultimately Hashem prevented him from carrying it out! So he had all levels of his consciousness crying out that this action could not be done, and Hashem said to him, in effect: "Yes, all that you feel and know is true, but kill him anyway!" *That* is a test! *That* is facing the impossible! And Abraham proceeded to do the impossible.

The result? The impossible occurred. Isaac was spared, he climbed down off the altar, and a ram was offered in his stead. But the *midrash* states: "The ashes of Isaac lie before Me"; in a higher dimension, he *was* sacrificed! Not the "ashes of the ram" but the "ashes of *Isaac.*" He became a pure burnt offering. The impossible paradox – a man who lives physically in this world, but spiritually in the next, *simultaneously!* And the qualities of father and son live on in the Jewish people – the ability to yield the emotions, the intellect, the entire personality to Hashem, and the gift of being able to live in a physical world and transcend it at the same time. They leave us the legacy of living this way, being moved by test after test to climb, to elevate the material to the spiritual and survive, miraculously. That father and son bring their potential into the actual, and more than that: they reach into the dimension of the impossible and bring *that* into the actual, and they give that to us. The Jewish people live the impossible; we begin where the impossible ends. We find hope beyond despair. And in essence, we have no limits.

DAVID AND BATSHEVA

What of David and Batsheva? What is the meaning of their relationship? What in fact was wrong with it? The *gemara* searches for an understanding of exactly where David sinned. The simple meaning of the words may be misleading – the *gemara* states that there was no sin of adultery or any other lowly error which may be read into the words. In fact Batsheva was destined for him, and from them was born

Solomon, the direct ancestor of the Messiah, not the likely outcome of that which was not meant to be.

David's error was that he *asked to be tested!* This needs understanding. What is wrong with asking for a test? If the purpose of life is to be tested, why should we not actively seek ordeals? But the answer lies in the very question. When one asks for a test one is asserting the confidence that one can succeed in the test: "Test me – I'll show you!" No-one asks for a test which he is certain to fail! No-one asks for a test which he believes lies in the realm of the utterly impossible!

And that confidence, that ego, that element of pride is just what *nisayon,* a test, comes to neutralize, to eliminate. A test is designed to awaken you to realize that you cannot do it alone, to awaken you to your relationship with Hashem. In the heroism of acting as you must despite the enormity of the challenge, in the very courage you display, you show the humility that it takes to admit that you need Him. To act when you know the result lies beyond your reach is to declare that He must be involved. To act when you know the result is beyond you is to admit your limitations, to state your humility.

So when David asked to be tested he manifested an infinitesimal degree of pride, at his supernal level. And the work which he is destined to do in the world is to show that he is nothing, that Hashem is everything, that the work which a Jew must do in the world is beyond natural ability, is in fact impossible.

Hashem carries us through. We act, but He accomplishes. For the man who is to teach this most powerful lesson to the Jewish people and the world even the smallest degree of asserting that he can do something independently of Hashem, as it were, is too much. Even though he had emptied himself of almost all vested interest, all ego, yet that tiny speck of pride was too much. And the only possible result, the solution in fact, was to fail. David's success was not yet to be; it must wait until the end of time, until the messianic revelation which will be manifest through him then.

ACHIEVE THE IMPOSSIBLE

We learn an exhilarating depth here. Ordeal leads to transcendence. In the paradox of facing crisis with a lion's strength and yet inwardly knowing that only Hashem manifests here, we reveal Him openly. What is possible and what is impossible is not our concern. The Alter of Kelm used to say: "Ask not if a thing is possible, ask only if it is necessary." Our concern is to rise to that partnership with the Divine which invites Him, as it were, to reach down to us.

So free will is the growth tool. The battleground is your soul, and your ordeals are the battles for conquest of your lower self. The task is to fight those battles and liberate the higher self that hides within you, and then to go beyond that: to *create* that which was beyond even your hidden self, and then to create it again, and to push beyond the very concept of limits.

That is Judaism, and that is you. Build yourself; create yourself. By developing your courage and your humility you rise to find and build a greater self.

Chapter 13

A Deeper Reality

How do you build faith in a dark world? How do you come to see that there is more to the world than meets the eye? How are you meant to relate to the idea of a higher world when that world cannot be seen from here? What evidence is there for a world after this? How do we sensitize ourselves to see beyond this world and this life?

Although the modern world does not demonstrate how to discover these things, and although it may seem impossible, Judaism has a formula for acquiring this knowledge. The world itself contains the evidence we need to become aware of what is beyond it, and the Torah indicates how that awareness is to be developed.

Let us study one line of thinking that leads in this direction.

Hashem has no physical form. He has no body, no physical substance, and no parts. The Rambam (Maimonides) states that one who believes that Hashem is physical or material has no share in the next world.

However, *the Torah speaks of Hashem as if He were physical* – many verses speak of His hand, His arm, His eyes and many other such attributes: "With a mighty hand and an outstretched arm"; "The eyes of Hashem...are upon it (the Land of Israel)." If we are forbidden to conceive of any physical or material image when relating to Hashem, why does the Torah do so?

We know that Hashem obeys His own rules, as it were; He observes the Torah's commandments – why not this one? How are we expected to relate to the Divine with no picture or image at all *when the Torah itself does*?

Attributing physical properties to Hashem is very serious indeed; one who prays to Hashem while picturing some image or form is transgressing this prohibition, and it is in the category of idolatry. Why then does the Torah, Hashem's own teaching, speak in graphic images? What exactly are you supposed to picture when reading verses which openly mention Hashem's hand or foot? And again, if it is forbidden to imagine a hand or a foot, why does the Torah express itself thus?

The Rambam himself deals with this problem. In the "Laws of the Fundamentals of Torah" he raises our question and answers: "The Torah speaks in human terms." This would appear to mean that the Torah is speaking metaphorically when it mentions Divine attributes in human terms; the Torah is "borrowing" human language. In other words, Hashem does not have a hand, but since we can only understand things within our experience the Torah speaks in terms familiar to us. We have a real hand, so when the Torah wishes to tell us about something too deep for us to understand directly, it uses the metaphor or analogy of a hand in order to convey its meaning to us.

At first glance it seems that the Torah speaks this way because we cannot understand any other method of expression; we can understand only those things which are part of our world. We live in a finite world; we are familiar with hands, eyes and feet – and therefore the Torah speaks to us in terms which are familiar to us. After all, how could the Torah speak in any other way and be understood by finite beings? Of course, we understand that beyond the metaphor, beyond the borrowed language, there is much more – the finite words of Torah clothe endless layers of deeper meaning; the outer layer is only the vehicle, so to speak, for the deeper meaning. But since abstraction cannot be expressed except through concrete means, the Torah speaks in those concrete terms which are familiar to us.

However, deeper thought will show that this cannot be correct. If the Rambam means that the Torah is using human terms as *mashal,* analogy, we are faced with two major difficulties. Firstly, how can the Torah speak in terms which are not strictly true? We know that the Torah is true in the very deepest sense possible; every nuance within Torah must be true. Since the Torah is none other than Hashem Himself speaking, even the outermost layers of its expression must be absolutely accurate and true.

Analogies and metaphors may be useful, but they are not true in themselves. An analogy describes something which can easily be understood in order to explain something more difficult; it may be a very successful way of explaining the more difficult thing *but it is not that thing*. If the Torah wants us to understand something very deep and abstract when it talks of Hashem's hand, how can it speak of a hand *if the simple meaning of that word is not literally true as well?* Put another way: if Hashem does not really have a hand, but the Torah says that He does because we are limited to finite and familiar concepts, is this not in some sense inaccurate, false? Is untruth justified because we cannot hear truth? Surely not!

And secondly, not only is it false to attribute physical properties to Hashem, it is forbidden! We are not allowed to conceive of Hashem as possessing any human or physical properties; why does the Torah apparently do just that? We are expected to relate to Hashem without imagining any finite form; why does the Torah describe such form? Does the forbidden become permitted because our minds are limited?

AN ANSWER

One way to approach our problem is this: when the Torah mentions attributes of Hashem such as His hand or His eye, it is referring to His conduct of the world and His actions within it. Understood thus, Hashem's hand would mean His actions within the physical realm, His eyes would mean that He sees what occurs in the world, and so on.

Now while this way of understanding our subject may be true, those sources which reach into the deepest realms of Torah thought indicate that it does not adequately solve our problem, and the reason is this: If Hashem's hand is understood to mean an action within the world, that is true only within the world. *However, the Torah indicates that Hashem Himself* has a hand; not only where His actions can be grasped by human awareness, but even far above the zone of our perception, as it were, in Hashem's Name of essence itself.

In other words, if the Torah talks of Hashem's hand, it *must* mean that He has a hand, intrinsically and most literally. It is not enough to say that the Torah is referring to something within the world when it mentions Divine attributes; the Torah's expression is clear: if it states that even above the finite world these things exist, it must be so. What does this mean?

A DEEPER ANSWER

We shall need to seek more deeply. There is a more accurate answer to our question, and one who understands it will experience a remarkable depth of perception.

Our question again: how can Hashem have a real hand? Surely a real hand is finite, physical, a contradiction to the infinite Oneness of the Creator? Surely the Divine hand must be some sort of *mashal*, analogy? But the secret which answers our question is this: *Hashem's hand is a real hand and our human hand is a mashal!* When the Torah talks of the Divine hand it is referring to that which is real in the deepest sense; that which is *infinite and no contradiction* to the absolute Oneness of the Creator. Every nuance of meaning in Torah is absolutely true; Hashem indeed has a hand – but that hand transcends human understanding no less than any other Divine attribute which is expressed in Torah, and no less than what we refer to as Hashem Himself.

Of course, this means that we cannot begin to understand any of the Divine attributes mentioned in the Torah. Since they all exist in that realm of Oneness which has no parts they do not contradict the idea of the Oneness of the Creator. And no human mind can begin to imagine the meaning of that which is described as specific or particular and yet does not contradict the idea of that Oneness.

So we can say that Hashem has a hand, but we cannot understand what that means. And that is exactly the point: *the reason that we have been created with hands is so that we can begin to understand!* We possess parts, components, aspects of our bodies so that we can begin to fathom the meaning of these things at their root. *We are the analogy!* Hashem wants us to begin to understand Him; part of the purpose of learning Torah is to begin to understand what a human can understand of the Divine, and therefore we are given the tangible tools that we need.

The Torah talks of reality, the highest reality. The Torah describes things *as they actually are;* but it uses human language – it uses language that refers to things in our world, things with which we are familiar so that we can begin to relate to those things that are above our world, those things that are real in the highest sense.

A WORLD OF EXAMPLES
In fact, this idea extends far beyond the human body: *the entire world is an analogy for a higher reality.* Each detail of the world teaches something about its source in the spiritual

dimension; each detail here is an exact parallel of that which exists there. This is perfectly logical: if we were commanded to study and understand the spiritual realm and yet had no avenue of access to that understanding, what would be the sense of such a command? The pathway to deeper insight is clear: we are meant to see more deeply, to look into those depths that cannot be seen by human eyes, and the way to do this is by means of a close and sensitive study of that which is revealed.

Just as you observe the physical body of your friend in order to relate to the *person* or inner being of that friend, so too you must study the structure and movements of the physical world in order to perceive its root. The truth is that there is no other way; you never see the inner being or *neshama,* soul, of another person – you have no sense-organ which can directly perceive a soul. All you can do is observe the person's body and its expression sensitively and you automatically gain insight into who they *are.* Subtle movements of the body, a subtle flicker of expression on the face, an almost imperceptible smile or motion, the slightest gesture of tension or relaxation in bodily posture – all of these speak worlds.

In fact, at those moments that are most critical and important in a relationship you may forget that there is a body – when a slight change of expression on your friend's face indicates that he has understood you perfectly and your friendship is deepened beyond the ability of words to describe, the last thing you are thinking of is the physical structure of his face and the muscles, nerves and skin that are moving to produce that change of expression. All of that is naturally translated by you into its inner meaning. The screen of the face is read in order to give you the content; the body transmits the soul so well that you feel you have seen the soul directly.

All communication between people occurs thus. Speech itself is nothing other than the physical moving of throat, tongue and lips generating sound waves which cause a physical response in the ear of the listener. The wonder is that subtle and refined ideas can be translated from their native medium in the mind and reduced to these physical forms. But there is no other way – the only access we have to the thoughts and personality of another human being is through the vehicle of the concrete, the physical.

In relating to people, that switch from outer body to inner person is achieved effortlessly: when you relate intensely to another person you are usually unaware of the interface provided by the body, you simply perceive the inner reality as if you are seeing it directly. This natural ability to use the medium of the body to see its core is a gift which teaches us that such perception can be achieved. *The challenge is to use the entire world in this way;* all aspects of the physical world should be observed and studied for what they reveal about their Creator.

This is a remarkable and inspiring view of the world: every object and experience it contains is a Divine lesson, a *mashal* relating to the Creator. He clothes Himself in a body which is the Universe and asks you to study that body carefully. And from each flicker of movement in that cosmic body you learn about Him. Just as you can perceive the human soul by means of its vehicle, the body, so too you can begin to perceive the Divine root of the world by means of that vehicle, that body which we call the world.

LIGHT PROJECTED

Once again, consider images projected on a screen: the forms and figures moving on the screen are no more than light dancing on a flat surface. They may look very convincing and you may even forget for a while that they are only pictures. But in fact those images are very distant versions of the people and places photographed to produce them. However, and this is the critical point to remember, *they are exact replicas of the original.*

They may be entirely illusory compared to their sources, but if you carefully study that light dancing on that screen *you will recognize those people and places when you meet them in the future.*

One who studies this world well is studying a distant reflection of a source which cannot be seen from here. But one day in the future, on that inevitable day when the transition must be made from this world to another, the one who has studied well will recognize every detail of reality. Then it will become apparent that this world, for all its beauty and sense of reality, is in depth a *mashal* for the higher world.

EXPERIENCE REFLECTS REALITY

Every human experience holds and teaches more than it seems to contain at first glance. Every human experience is the finite translation of an infinite idea. Human consciousness, while locked into a physical body, interprets deeper experience as superficial experience; our work is to translate that superficial experience back into its source in depth.

Every experience in life is given in order for us to learn about the higher world. Every experience here is an expression of a deeper experience in the spiritual dimension. Every experience here is a learning exercise in developing an understanding of the higher world, a projection on the screen of our bodies and emotions.

You can gain a unique insight into the world by examining all of human experience in the light of this idea. Why do we laugh? Why do we cry? Why do we long to travel and yet long for home when we are away? Each of these experiences, in fact every detail of human behavior and response, reveals a source in the soul.

Perhaps one or two examples will illustrate the point.

Why do we long for home? It is a universal human experience that when one is away from one's home, and particularly from the home of one's youth, one longs to be back there. A place has special beauty in the eyes of those who live there, even when that place has no particular natural beauty. "A place has special beauty for those who live in it." If all of our experiences are none other than this-worldly parallels of higher experiences, what does this mean?

The answer is that the *neshama,* the soul, is derived from a higher world; its true place, its true home, is that world where it enjoyed indescribable closeness with its Creator. It is sent into this world, immeasurably distant from that place of origin, into the body of a mortal being. But it never forgets its home; it forever longs with a most powerful longing to return. However, this depth remains subconscious; the *neshama* longs for its real home in the spiritual realm but the emotions read that longing as homesickness! After all, the realm of origin is not visible from here; the *neshama* has lost sight of it, the mind cannot see it. And so the conscious mind interprets that deep experience of origin as a particular human experience familiar to each of us.

And when we are home we long to travel! Despite the *neshama's* love of its origin, it nevertheless longs to move through this world, distant from its home, to enjoy the beauty of this world and to acquire its wealth – the true wealth of good deeds and perfection of character. That is the origin of the desire to travel; the conscious mind experiences this deep stirring of the *neshama* as wanderlust, the longing to travel.

Each facet of human behavior and emotion must be studied closely for the clues it holds. No part of the mind or the world is accidental or coincidental. If the world is a projection of a deeper reality, then each detail reveals the reality that projects it.

And all of this is to give us the clues we need to uncover origins; our own, and those of the entire world.

ILLUSION WITHIN ILLUSION

So we understand that all our experiences are projections of reality which teach us about that reality. All our experiences teach us something about reality from within the world of illusion. But if this is true, we must face a perplexing question: if every human experience is an illusion relative to its source in the higher world, *what is a dream?* What does a dream teach us about reality? If our experiences here are illusions relative to their source in the higher world, why would Hashem create us with dreams as part of our lives – a dream is all illusion; why put illusion into the illusion?

Let us understand: in a dream, you are not aware that you are dreaming – the dream seems very real, sometimes ecstatically pleasurable, sometimes terrifyingly traumatic. The very intensity of these feelings is due to the fact that you perceive them as fully alive and real. And yet when you wake, sitting up in bed in a sweat generated by the torment of a nightmare, you are relieved to realize that what you have just gone through was only a dream. Why do we need this experience of the unreal which seems so real?

The answer is clear and illuminating. Imagine for a moment an uninformed person being told about the nature of life in this world and the transition from this world to the next. Imagine that such a person is told: "Know that this world is only an illusion relative to the next. It may seem real, but do not be fooled – one day, sooner or later, you will leave this dimension and enter an entirely different one. There you will realize that all you have experienced in life was a very faint echo of the reality you will perceive there. That is real life; whatever you knew before was almost nothing in comparison to it."

The person being told this story would probably reply: "That sounds wild! How can I accept such an idea? Surely it is more reasonable for me to see the world as it meets the eye right now; how can I believe that all my awareness of the world is only an illusion? That is simply outside of my experience and outside of all the evidence available to me. I reject such fanciful and unsubstantiated stories!"

And he would certainly be excused for replying thus! A person could not be expected to doubt his perception of the world with which he has such solid contact. Since all his senses assure him that his experience of the world is true and reliable, he could not think otherwise.

Unless he has ever had a dream! Anyone who has ever dreamed has *experienced* the remarkable transition from what seems completely real to a state in which it is obvious that the reality of which he was so sure a few seconds before was entirely an illusion! After living through a few vivid dreams a person *must* be faced with a very unsettling thought: when you dream, let us say a terrifying dream, and you awake and sit upright in bed still sweating and shaking, you are enormously relieved to realize that it was only a dream and that now you are awake. *But are you sure*? Can you be sure? How do you know that you are awake now – because you simply know, you can feel clearly that you are awake? But in your dream you were certain that you were awake too!

Hashem wants us to know about this world and the next. He wants us to realize that this life is temporary and will end in a transition to a totally different existence. He wants us to realize that this reality is not forever even though it may seem so. How can He teach us this? How can He convince you that what you experience now is not reliable, that your perception is not guaranteed to be accurate? The answer is: go to sleep! Go to sleep and after one dream you will know. After one dream in which you go through ecstasy or agony, one dream in which you experience what seems to be a clear reality, so clear that your heart beats in panic and you shake with terror, and then you wake and realize that what you went through only a moment before was all an illusion, you will know *deeply and thoroughly* that your perception of reality is not reliable. You will know that there is no assurance that this world and your life within it are solid and eternally unchanging. You will have been sensitized; you will have been awakened in the deepest sense possible. If you have any spiritual potential at all you will have learned life's most important lesson.

A dream has taught you about reality; sleep has woken you.

Anyone who has dreamed has experienced the priceless gift of feeling in the flesh, in the most immediate way, that the state of being which we call life in this world has no assurance of being real or permanent. The briefest dream kills forever the smug self-assurance that would otherwise be natural – the confidence that your experience is perfectly reliable and that you experience the only reality that there is. A dream is a humbling experience. And it is the key to belief in a world after this; it is an experience in this world that should sensitize you to the idea that there is more to life here than meets the eye. No one who has dreamed can possibly deny that with any confidence at all.

And so even a dream, that experience of illusion, teaches about reality! Dreams do not break the rule: every human experience is an opportunity to learn about reality.

Epilogue

Straw and Fire

The Jewish people are likened to fire and flame, and our enemies are likened to straw. We and the Torah that lives within us are fire; the world around us and its materialism are straw.

Torah is the point of connection with the world of spirit. It is the spark of an infinite flame, burning in a world of the finite and the superficial. The Torah itself states: "And the house of Jacob shall be fire, and the house of Joseph flame, and the house of Esau shall be straw." What exactly is the meaning of this comparison?

The Midrash gives an analogy. There was once a pechami – a seller of coals in the marketplace (in the ancient world, one would buy coals to light one's home fires – the pechami kept coals alight and glowing for sale.) A straw merchant arrived in the same marketplace and began piling up his bales of straw. After a while there was no place to move, and the pechami became afraid. Tons of straw were filling the market and there was no place left.

At that point, a wise man who was present spoke to the pechami: "What are you afraid of? When his straw gets too close to your fire, one spark from your coals will end the problem!"

This Midrash teaches a fundamental lesson about the Jewish people and the Torah in the long battle against the external forces which seek to destroy us. The Esau-nations, their culture and their values are represented by straw: straw has only one kind of value, and that lies in quantity. A few pieces of straw are worthless; only in bulk does straw achieve value. Its worth is proportional to its mass. Those nations and cultures which oppose the spiritual, value the material, and the material has value in its mass; he who has more is wealthier. When Esau comes to meet Jacob he proclaims his wealth: "I have much." His wealth lies in the sheer volume and mass of his possessions – "I have much." These nations would swamp the Jewish people if they could, eliminate us and our historical commitment to spiritual values, and establish a world unfettered by moral niceties and considerations of the spiritual; in fact, they would gladly use their bulk and might to destroy Jacob.

Jacob, on the other hand, meets his brother's declaration of wealth with: "For I have everything." Spiritual values live on a plane above mass and volume, and none of the terms relating to mass or bulk are relevant – "I have everything." Completeness is not possible in the realm of the physical, but above that realm it becomes natural.

Jewish values do not consist of mass or bulk. We do not seek to have "much", we do not define wealth in terms of "more". Our idea of wealth and value lies in the domain of completeness; you are wealthy when you have *enough*, when you are complete within yourself, when you lack nothing. We seek completeness, perfection of the self. *We seek quality, not quantity.*

And that is why Jacob is likened to fire. Straw achieves value in bulk, but fire is fire no matter how little of it there is. One spark is enough to ignite a whole world of straw; and in that final and inevitable battle between the might of muscle and the light of genuine spirit, it is the small spark of real fire which will prevail. When the bales of straw, that substance which is nothing but the outer layer of the wheat within, pile up and threaten the lone coal-seller and his embers, one tiny spark from those embers will set the world ablaze and all externality and superficiality will be transformed into light.

But there is one requirement for this: the coals must retain their fire. Quantity is irrelevant, but quality is everything – if the coals harbor even one genuine spark, all will be well. But if the fire dies, then what is left is worth even less than straw.

So guard your coals. In the marketplace of the world where lifestyles and values come and go, where might and power threaten to drown the light of spirit, guard your coals. When the world forgets its humanity and Torah seems irrelevant, make sure that in your heart there is genuine spark and flame.